ITALIAN · FRENCH · SPANISH · GERMAN

Phonetics and Diction in Singing

by Kurt Adler

UNIVERSITY OF MINNESOTA PRESS · MINNEAPOLIS

Second printing, 1974

This book is based on Chapters 4–8 of Mr. Adler's
The Art of Accompanying and Coaching

ISBN 0-8166-0446-0

Preface

MY BOOK *The Art of Accompanying and Coaching* has been out for only about two years. It fell upon fertile soil, and during the long period consumed by its writing and its preparation for printing the musical climate in America grew considerably warmer.

What one of the less offensive clichés of our day calls a cultural explosion is taking place in this country. Opportunities for singers, in concert as well as in opera, are multiplying in universities, colleges, high schools, workshops, and music groups. More young people are listening to good music, many FM radio stations are broadcasting serious music around the clock, and even television networks sometimes weather the storm of advertising agencies and sneak in some long-hair musical programs. Politicians have discovered the publicity value of being seen at musical performances; the big foundations and even some giants of industry and business are spending enormous amounts of money to encourage the development of music. American cities that have heretofore been dependent on touring opera groups to satisfy their cultural needs are proudly forming their own opera companies and groups. Germany's, Austria's, and Switzerland's opera houses simply could not exist without young American singers, because their own strength in this field has not yet been restored to pre-war standards. Thus the United States, once a country that imported foreign musical talent, is now exporting its own cultural products. Given all necessary training, a young artist — with good advisory guidance — will be able to have a career in this country without having to make the expensive detour through Europe that was almost obligatory in earlier years.

This all means that the number of voice students and necessarily also the number of voice teachers is increasing from year to year. It is not an exaggeration to say that we are already experiencing a shortage of well-prepared, talented young singers who are ready to step into the breach caused by the evergrowing number of possibilities for professional engagements.

From its first pages, my book was slanted not only toward accompanists and coaches — although these were its principal audience, since it is the only textbook of its kind — but also toward the whole "vocal population" of this country. The success of the book demonstrated the good sense of my approach. Reports came in from all sides to suggest that voice teachers and students in great numbers were perusing my book. These reports also told me that the chapters on phonetics and diction were especially helpful, because they contain all the rules and examples necessary for the study of songs and opera in the leading foreign tongues.

One may ask why phonetics and diction in Italian, Latin, French, Spanish, and German are essential in a country where the trend is toward opera in English. The answer is simple: if you know how to sing well in these languages and know how to apply the rules correctly you will also sing well in English. I have emphasized many times that singing diction is quite different from diction in speech. English is rich in diphthongs which if pronounced in singing exactly as they are in speech would make the voice sound uneven, mushy, devoid of the beauty of bel canto. The study of foreign operatic and song literature in its native tongues will provide the correct basis for a sound vocal technique. The application of that sound technique to English, combined with the right way of projection, will help the English-speaking singing student and artist considerably, even decisively.

Although I want to refrain from discussing the basic rules for English phonetics and singing diction, leaving it to qualified American-born experts, I must caution against misconstruing my words to make them suggest that the result of using this system would make English sound as it sometimes does — especially in our big opera houses: almost completely unintelligible. The reason for this deplorable fact is again the impossibility of singing English the way you pronounce it in speech. There are many English diction teachers, some of them actors or Shakespearian experts, who destroy any vocal phrase by teaching the "sing as you speak" method. Only a good coach or a teacher who not only knows the correct pronunciation but also thoroughly understands how to adapt it to the vocal problems of phonetics and diction can show young artists the proper English singing diction. But even these professional teachers will have to consult dictionaries or other source material when they deal with foreign languages and, should they encounter especially difficult problems — as for instance when to make a liaison in singing French — even these sources might not give satisfactory and authoritative solutions.

This book, composed of the chapters on phonetics and diction from my larger book, *The Art of Accompanying and Coaching*, is intended to do just that. These chapters form a handbook and a textbook based on my many years of experience in which I have tried to meet every foreseeable problem. It is therefore completely accurate to substitute "voice teacher and singer" for "accompanist and coach" whenever you come upon the latter. A serious student of this book ought to be able to teach himself the mechanics of phonetics and diction in singing, and at the professional level the book may be used as a reference work, to check up on questions in doubt or to find exceptions to a rule. A voice teacher and coach performing a supervisory and constructively critical function will of course be beneficial even to the student well along the road toward professionalism.

In publishing the phonetics and diction chapters from *The Art of Accompanying and Coaching* separately I feel certain that a wider circle of vocalists will be reached; many of them will also be interested in learning about the other important ingredients that go into the making of an artist — and they may be led back to the larger work.

KURT ADLER

Table of Contents

PHONETICS AND DICTION IN SINGING

Phonetics and Diction in Singing

WHICH is more important, the words or the music? To this day, the old argument has lost nothing of its ardor, its vehemence, its partisanship, and above all its emotional aspects and its question mark.

Truly, which of the two arts is more important when combined in a vocal composition? The question has occupied many great creative artists and many of their utterances about this problem could be quoted. But it may be best to let a great musician take the rostrum. At an age when wisdom and experience become molded into serene impartiality, Richard Strauss undertook to cast this ever-alive question into poetic and musical form. His conversation piece for music, *Cappriccio*, has this problem as its main topic. He lets a poet and a musician argue the question, fight about it, and finally leave it to a beautiful woman of noble heart and soul to solve. Though Strauss leaves the question unan-

swered — the opera ends without the solution's actually being announced — by his words "music and word are brother and sister" he leaves no doubt in anybody's mind that the fight must end in a draw. In vocal art the word is lifted up and ennobled by the music, the music is made clear and brought into focus by the word. This chapter will analyze the elements of the spoken word and discuss their adjustment to the singing phrase.

It has been said that in vocal art the singing comes from the heart, but the words must be controlled by the intellect. This is only partly true. Both music and words must come from the heart, but both must also be controlled by the brain — not only controlled but brought under a common denominator which could be called the esthetic golden mean.

A word consists of sounds. The science of producing and pronouncing sounds is called phonetics; the enunciation of words and sentences synthesized from sounds is called diction. Spoken and sung sounds fall into the categories of vowels, semivowels, vowel combinations (diphthongs, triphthongs), and consonants.

The popular belief that there are five different vowels has been discarded by the science of phonetics. Of the languages most frequently encountered in vocal literature, Italian has seven vowels, German fourteen, English fifteen, and French sixteen. When we come to vowel combinations and consonants, the confusion grows even greater.

The International Phonetic Alphabet (IPA), created in 1888 and revised in 1951, has a sign for each sound. This alphabet may be too complicated for every singer to learn, but it is a necessity for accompanists and coaches who want to master the intricacies of phonetics and diction for singers. This book will use the IPA because of its definitiveness and because it allows no error and no second meaning of a sound. It will then be up to the individual accompanist or coach to judge the intelligence of his singers and use any method of making the sound clear to them.

The comparative simplicity of Italian, as suggested by its use of only seven vowels, makes it the easiest language to sing. It therefore will be the first language to be discussed and its vowels will form the basis for those of all other languages with which singers should be familiar, at least phonetically.

The accompanist and coach with aspirations must know one Romance language well enough to be able to converse fluently, in addition to thoroughly understanding its phonetical, grammatical, and stylistic intricacies. Since Italian is easier than French, the American coach or accompanist will have fewer difficulties in speaking Italian than French. Besides this complete mastery of one Romance language, a thorough knowledge of another one, as well as of German, is essential. The accompanist or coach must understand these languages from the point of view of all their phonetic and linguistic problems. This seems a very high standard, but we must keep in mind what I said in the introductory chapter about the qualifications and background of an accompanist or coach. If he is able to thoroughly search one language for its philological qualities he will be in a much better position to study and understand other languages. As a famous linguist who was proficient in about sixty-four languages once said: "Only the first six are difficult; after that, everything becomes very easy."

This book is meant for American and English accompanists and coaches. Complete knowledge of English is an assumed prerequisite. Although it is a known fact that English singing diction is frequently massacred by coaches as well as by singers, this book will not undertake to analyze faulty production and enunciation of English phrases. A very good book, *The Singer's Manual of English Diction* by Madeleine Marshall (published by G. Schirmer's, Inc., New York), is available and should not be absent from any accompanist's or coach's studio. Where my experience with singers has led me to different conclusions from Miss Marshall's, my point of view will be offered.

These chapters will make Italian, Latin, French, Spanish, and German singing diction understandable to accompanists and coaches. The problems which will be brought into focus must necessarily be based on the relation of the pronunciation of these languages to the pronunciation of native tongue of teacher and student, namely, English.

I purposely use the term "singing diction." This book is not concerned with speech as such and the elements of speech are treated only as they are related to singing. One of the most widespread errors is that spoken and sung sounds are the same. Nothing is further from the truth. To sing the way you speak may be advisable for popular music, but it would make the voice sound brittle, harsh, and uneven in opera, song, and choral music. The adjustment of phonetics to the vocal phrase is the real problem for any accompanist and coach and the solution constitutes a very important part of his art. The basic elements of phonetics are nevertheless the speech sounds and this chapter will start with them. Of the speech sounds, the vowels are the simplest.

A vowel is a voiced speech sound which originates in the larynx and passes unhindered through the channel formed by throat and mouth. Different vowels will require different positions of the speech apparatus, but in all vowels the passage through throat and mouth is uninterrupted by obstacles. Obstacles to the speech sounds

Symbol	Italian	French	Spanish	German	English
			VOWELS		
[a]	patria	pâle, pas, patte	pan	fahren, Gast	far
[ɛ]	vendetta, pesca (peach)	tête, mère	escuela, cerca	Bett, Bär	pet
[e]	era, pesca (fishing)	thé		leben	chaotic (approx.)
[ə]		ville		Erde	about, herb (approx.)
[i]	si	si	sì	wie, bitte	see, bit
[o]	dove	beau	llorar	wohl	
[ɔ]	cosa	porte, fort	ojo	Sonne	Scotch, fought
[ø]		peu		schön	
[œ]		oeuf, veuve		zwölf	surf, sir (approx.)
[u]	subito	tout	mucho	gut, Hund	doom, book (approx.)
[y]		lune		über, Glück	
[ɑ̃]		ange, ensemble			
[ɛ̃]		infame, teint			
[ɔ̃]		ombre, onde			
[œ̃]		un, humble			
			SEMIVOWELS		
[w]	quando	oiseau, oui	cuando, huelga	ew'ge, Jahr	suave, persuasion
[j]	ieri	hier	tibio		you, yet
[ɥ]		puis, huit			
			CONSONANTS		
[b]	bene	bien	bueno	Bett	bet
[β]			hablar		love (Southern U.S., approx.)
[ç]			yo (in stress)	ich	hue (in stress)

IPA	Italian	French	Spanish	German	English
[θ]			corazon, cinco		thunder
[f]	forte	fort	fuerte	fast	fast
[g]	gamba	guérir	guerra	gerne	get
[gs]		exil			exile
[y]			luego		
[h]		haine		hoch	high
[k]	caro	carte	calidad	kalt	cold
[ks]		luxe	excavar	Luchs	lax
[l]	lungo	long	leche	lachen	
[ʎ]	figlia		llamar (Castilian)		
[j]		fille	llamar (Mexican)	Joch	yonder
[m]	amore	amour	amor	Mann	man
[n]	onda	nez	andar	Name	name
[ɲ]	agnus	agneau	señor		onion
[ŋ]	angolo		cinco, tengo	singen	sing
[p]	padre	père	padre	Pore	pour
[r]	rosso	rouge	rojo	rot	red
[s]	sangue	sang	sangre	rasten	see
[z]	sdegno	zèle	rasgar	Sohn	zeal
[dz]	zero				adze
[ʒ]		jour	alli (Argentinian)	Gendarm	vision, measure
[dʒ]	giubilo				jar
[ʃ]	scioccc	chaud		schön	show
[t]	tutto	tout	todo	Tonne	tan
[ts]	zio			Zahn	Tsar
[tʃ]	cielo	caoutchouc	charro	rutschen	church
[v]	verde	vert	verde	warm	vast
[x]			gente, jabon	Loch	khan, loch

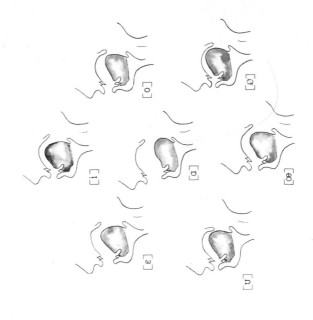

Figure 18. Mouth positions during the production of the principal kinds of vowel sound

come into play in helping to form the other speech sounds, the consonants. Vowels' unobstructed passage makes them the foremost carriers of the singing tone. A simple example will illustrate this: The vocalise in its voice-building form in a teacher's studio and in its adaptation as a special vocal art form (see Ravel's or Rachmaninoff's Vocalise) consists entirely of a vowel or vowels. Any examination of singing phonetics and diction must therefore start with the vowel speech sounds; this I shall follow, for each language, with a discussion of semivowels, combinations of vowels (such as diphthongs and triphthongs), and consonants.

CLASSIFICATION OF VOWELS

The vowels can be classified in many ways. The easiest way is to divide them into front, middle, and back, a division based on different positions of tongue and lips.

Vowels can also be divided into a long and closed or short and open vowel. The most natural vowel is the a which is the least modified vowel. According to William Vennard, "The pharynx is distended comfortably, the jaw is dropped, the tongue is low and grooved, if possible."

e and i are formed by slight changes of the tongue position, o and u by progressive rounding of the lips.

Figure 18 shows simplifications of X-rays of tones, as illustrated in G. Oscar Russell's book, *Speech and*

Voice. This should help to give the accompanist and coach an idea of the changes in the mouth when different vowels are pronounced. Figure 19 may make the relative position of the Italian, French, and German vowels more understandable. The difference in production between long and short vowels is neglected in Figure 18.

CLASSIFICATION OF CONSONANTS

The consonants are produced by actually putting obstacles in the way of the free flow of the air stream, which deflects, hinders, or interrupts it. If the vowels can be considered the flesh of the sound body, the consonants are the bones that hold the flesh together. There are several possible systems for the classification of consonants.

Some consonants are *voiced*; this means that they carry with them some remnants of voice sound. Others are *voiceless*; they do not contain voice sound at all. You can "hear" the voiced consonants if you cover your ears and softly articulate [b], [d], [g], [v], and [z]. Using

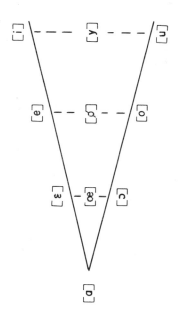

Figure 19. Diagram showing relative positions of Italian, French, and German vowels

the same method, you will "hear" nothing while articulating [p], [t], [k], [f], [s], and [ʃ].

Moreover, the consonants can be classified by the location of the speech apparatus in which they are produced. This most widely accepted classification contains the glottal fricative sound, the [h] which is aspirated in the larynx; the labial sounds, produced by the lips, called bilabials if both lips are involved (p and b) and labiodentals if upper teeth and lower lip are used in producing these sounds (f and v). Bilabials and labiodentals are either voiced (b and v) or voiceless (p and f).

Yet another method of classification takes into consideration the degree of freedom from obstruction of the air stream in forming consonants. If the obstruction is total, we talk of plosives. Their release requires a slight explosion of the accumulated air pressure. Consonants of this type are [b], [p], [d], [t], [g], and [k]. If the obstruction is not complete but leaves a narrow channel open in which the articulated consonants rub against the channel's borders, we speak of fricative sounds, such as [f], [v], [θ], [ð], [ʃ], [ʒ], and [h].

The other consonants cannot be produced without the aid of the tongue. They are therefore called *linguals*. If tongue and upper gum ridge are involved in producing consonants, their name is lingua-alveolars. Such consonants are [d] (voiced) and [t] (voiceless). By slight modification of the tongue (letting some breath escape through a slight contact between tongue and upper teeth) we get the [s] (voiceless) and the [z] (voiced). Further modifications of this are the [ʃ] (voiceless) and the [ʒ] (voiced), produced by withdrawing the tongue a little from the alveolar ridge. [g] (voiced) and [k] (voiceless) are velar consonants, produced by a meeting of the back of the tongue and the soft palate.

Of the nasal sounds, [m] is a bilabial nasal, produced by closing the lips; [n] is an alveolar nasal, made by pressing the forward part of the tongue against the upper gum ridge. [ŋ] is a velar nasal effected by pressing the middle part of the tongue against the hard palate. For all those the velum should be arched, unless a French nasal sound is desired, in which case the velum is somewhat lowered. Those consonants which belong to French or German only will be described in their proper place.

A special discussion is needed for the [l] which is either *dental-alveolar* (as in Italian, French, and German), or more *guttural* (as in English). Some Slavic languages have both of these l's and use different signs for them: ł for the guttural (hard) and l for the dental (soft) [l] in Russian and in Polish.

There are four ways to articulate the [r]. Firstly, it can be flipped by a slight trill of the tip of the tongue against the upper gum ridge. This is the Italian or French (in singing) and English alveolar [r]. Secondly, it can be rolled by a flutter of the soft palate against the back of the tongue. This is the German and Slavic r and with a lesser roll it appears also in the speech of the French, especially Parisians (but should not be used in singing). The third kind of r is the English way of articulating it by curling the tip of the tongue upward and slightly backward toward the region of the alveolar ridge and hard palate and returning very fast to its initial position. The fourth way is typically American, pronounced very sloppily.

The production and pronunciation of semivowels, diphthongs, triphthongs, and consonant combinations will be discussed in the paragraphs concerning the individual languages to which they belong.

Italian Phonetics and Diction

I HAVE said before that the Italian needs only seven different vowel sounds to form words and sentences in his language. These vowel sounds are the purest of any language. This purity, free from any disfiguring diphthongization, is the main reason for the undisputed position of Italian as the most musical language in the world. Vowels are only infrequently interspersed with consonants. Diphthongization is practically unknown. All this creates the basis for the bel canto style of singing which is predominant today in America. It is quite possible to adjust even French and German words to this style of singing. The seven Italian vowels are shown in Figure 20. Most of these vowels are long. They are short — but not necessarily open — only before a double consonant. This is true only of Italian, which is the sole language where the shortening of a vowel does not automatically mean the opening of that vowel.

Cond[ɔ]tta ell' era in c[e]ppi (VERDI *Il Trovatore*)
Povero Rigol[e]tto (VERDI *Rigoletto*)
Buon giorno, Marc[ɛ]llo (PUCCINI *La Bohème*)

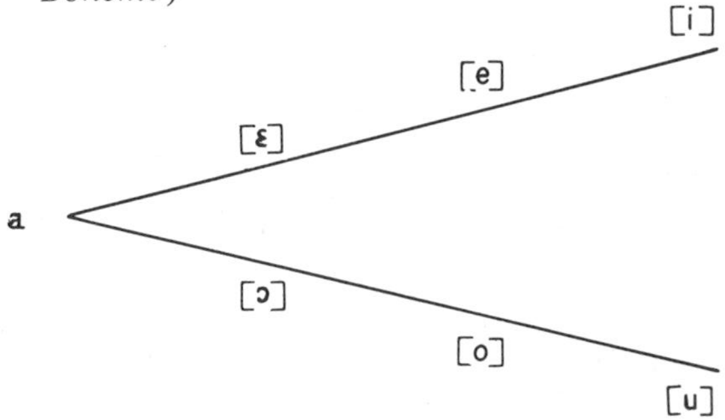

Figure 20. The seven Italian vowels

The [a] *sound.* The pronunciation of the Italian a is similar to the Boston way of saying father. The a is always bright, except when vocal blending asks for dark-

[12]

ening or adjustment of the vowel. In producing it the tongue should be relaxed and grooved, its tip lightly anchored on the lower teeth ridge.

a can be either long or short. It is long in an accentuated syllable, before another vowel or a single consonant, and always short if not accentuated, or before more than one consonant.

Āmāmi, oh Álfredo! (VERDI *La Traviata*)
All' ārmi! (VERDI *Il Trovatore*)

a gets a grave accent if it is the final letter of a word and supposed to be stressed. It is always long.

Ābbiāte cārità! (VERDI *La Forza del Destino*)
Pietà di me, pietà, Signor! (VERDI *La Forza del Destino*)

The [ɛ] *sound.* The [ɛ] corresponds exactly to the sound in the English words *bed, set, letter.* In singing, the [ɛ] is always open when it is the final sound of a word or if it falls on an unaccentuated syllable of a polysyllabic word.

E a parlar[ɛ], mi sforza d'amor[ɛ] (MOZART *Le Nozze di Figaro*)
L[ɛ] d[ɛ]lizi[ɛ] d[ɛ]ll' amor (VERDI *Rigoletto*)

In the following words the final e is *closed: chè* (and combinations, such as *perchè, poicchè,* etc.) *tre* (and combinations), *me, te,* and *se* if stressed; *re; nè; mercè, verdè* (and other 3rd person singular forms of the absolute past of verbs on *-ere*).

In accented syllables of a polysyllabic word the e can be either open or closed. This is also true if the e precedes a double consonant. No hard and fast rule can be established concerning where to use open or short e's; the accompanist or coach will have to look up the word in a good dictionary.

Si, v[ɛ]nd[ɛ]tta, tr[ɛ]m[ɛ]nda v[ɛ]nd[ɛ]tta (VERDI *Rigoletto*)
S[ɛ]mpr[ɛ] lib[ɛ]ra d[ɛ]ggio foll[ɛ]ggiar[ɛ] (VERDI *La Traviata*)

Sometimes words spelled identically have different meanings, depending upon whether the e is pronounced open or closed.

V[e]nti scudi nè da di prodotto (VERDI *Rigoletto*)
La calunnia è un v[ɛ]ntic[ɛ]llo (ROSSINI *Il Barbiere di Siviglia*)
La l[e]gge, io non la sò (PUCCINI *Madama Butterfly*)
Ei l[ɛ]gge, non vi parla (VERDI *Otello*)

Some suffixes with e on stressed syllables are short, as in frat-[ε]llo, sor-[ε]lla, -[ε]nte, -[ε]simo, and -[ε]stre.

Att[e]ndi, frat[e]llo (VERDI *Rigoletto*)
Buon giorno, sor[e]llina (DONIZETTI *Don Pasquale*)
De miei boll[ε]nti spiriti (VERDI *La Traviata*)

The e with grave accent is always pronounced [ε], with the exception of the examples above.

The [e] (closed e) *sound.* There are fewer [e]'s in Italian than [ε]'s. The e is closed in some accented syllables of a polysyllabic word, sometimes even before a double consonant.

O monum[e]nto (PONCHIELLI *La Gioconda*)
Povero Rigol[e]tto (VERDI *Rigoletto*)

The sound in e or ed (and) is always long and closed. Some monosyllabic words and some e's with grave accents have the closed sound. (See note above.)

Eh or deh (exclamation) is closed as the stretching h indicates.

Stressed e's in suffixes are closed, as in diminutives with -etto and -etta, and in forms with -ese, -essa, -evole, -ezza, -mente.

Caro il mio Figar[e]tto (MOZART *Le Nozze di Figaro*)

Susan[e]tta, sei tu (MOZART *Le Nozze di Figaro*)
Cont[e]ssa, perdono (MOZART *Le Nozze di Figaro*)
All' uso Giappon[e]s[ε] (PUCCINI *Madama Butterfly*)
L[ε]gg[ε]rm[e]nt[ε], dolc[ε]m[e]nt[ε]. (ROSSINI *Il Barbiere di Siviglia*)

The contraction de'e (from deve) is pronounced [dee].

Both e and ε sounds may have to be modified toward [ø] and [œ] if the vocal line demands it.

The i *sound.* The i sound in Italian is almost always long and is pronounced in exactly the same way as the vowels in the English words sea, see, relieve, feeling, and key. Double consonants following the i do not shorten it, but final i's are usually short. The i has four different functions. It can be syllabic (dominating a syllable):

Vissi d'arte (PUCCINI *Tosca*)

It can be asyllabic (unaccented):

Poi mi guidavi ai fulgidi deserti (VERDI *Otello*)

It can serve as a semivowel:

è miele o fiele (PUCCINI *La Bohème*)

[14]

It can be mute, and it remains unpronounced in the following combinations cia, cie, cio, ciu, gia, gie, gio, giu, scia, scie, scio, sciu, glie, glio, gliu:

mi lascio reggere prima di cedere farò giocar (ROSSINI Il Barbiere di Siviglia)

The i is pronounced in scienza, usually spelled scïenza.

Con scenica scïenza (PUCCINI Tosca)

ii is pronounced and sung like one prolonged i.

Fugii pur ora da Castel' Sant'Angelo (PUCCINI Tosca)

The i in its pure form tends to sound shrill and metallic, especially in top tones. It is advisable to produce the i sound without spreading the lips, or "smiling." The tip of the tongue should again be anchored against the lower teeth ridge. The forward part of the tongue has to arch upward but should not move too high, otherwise it would make the forward cavity of the mouth too small. While the pure metallic i used to be acceptable in provincial Italian opera houses, the great singers of La Scala always modified it toward [e] or [y]. It will be up to the accompanist and coach to discourage spreading the i and to blend it with the rest of the vowels in a musical phrase.

The y in Italian appears mostly in words of Greek derivation and is pronounced like i. It is always a pure vowel and not, as sometimes in English, a semiconsonant.

The [ɔ] (open o) sound. The [ɔ] sound in Italian is similar to the English o in provide. It is produced by rounding the lips and lowering the jaw, keeping the cavity of the mouth open and round, and the position of the tongue low. The tendency to diphthongization must be avoided. The lips must be rounded but should not protrude much since this would result in a closed o. German equivalents are S[ɔ]nne, R[ɔ]ss; French equivalents are d[ɔ]rner, t[ɔ]rt.

The o in Italian is always pronounced [ɔ] if it is the final sound of a word or if it falls on the unaccented syllable of a polysyllabic word.

Un cert[ɔ] n[ɔ]n s[ɔ] che (VIVALDI "Song")
Or che mi c[ɔ]n[ɔ]scete (PUCCINI *La Bohème*)

In monosyllabic words the o is always pronounced [ɔ], as in non, con, don.

The o in accented syllables of polysyllabic words may be either open or closed. A non-Italian must look up each such word in the dictionary.

La d[ɔ]nna è m[ɔ]bile (VERDI *Rigoletto*)
P[ɔ]c[ɔ], p[ɔ]c[ɔ] (PUCCINI *La Bohème*)

The o is pronounced [ɔ] before ll, mm, nn, rr, ss, or zz. It can be open or closed before tt. "Oh" as an exclamation is pronounced [ɔ].

[ɔ], quant[ɔ] è bella (VERDI *Rigoletto*)

The ò (with grave accent) is also always pronounced [ɔ]. The accent indicates only the stress of the word and does not change the sound.

L'amer[ɔ], sar[ɔ] c[ɔ]stante (MOZART *Il Re Pastore*)
M[ɔ]rr[ɔ] (VERDI *La Traviata*)

The [o] (closed o) *sound.* The [o] has no equivalent in English. All similar sounds, as in cold, low, are diphthongized. The [o] is equivalent to the German so, wo, hoch, or the French eau, or rose. The best way of finding the right production for the [o] is to produce an Italian a and round the lips while holding it. While the lips are gradually rounded, the vowel change runs from a bright [a] to a covered [a] and thence through different shades to an [o]. All these shades of [a] and [o] are important for the singer in blending vowels and evening out vocal coloring.

Another approach for an accompanist or coach to use in showing the English-speaking singer how to produce a pure [o] would be to analyze the production of an English (diphthongized) o, as in no, so. It starts the same way as the pure [o] – with rounded lips. The lips, however, are relaxed as the diphthongization progresses until the sound approaches a [u] (no = no-u, so = so-u). By pronouncing these words very slowly and arresting the rounded lips on the first part without proceeding to the [u] sound, the first part then is the pure [o] sound.

The cavity of the mouth should be fully utilized for the resonance of the [o] by keeping the palate high and the tongue low, the latter again lightly anchored on the lower teeth ridge. The jaw is less dropped than in pronouncing the open o. The o is closed in some accented syllables of a polysyllabic word but a dictionary must be used to determine exactly which o is open and which closed. Sometimes an o is closed even before a double consonant.

C[ɔ]nd[o]tta ell' era in ceppi (VERDI *Il Trovatore*)
BUT: alla l[ɔ]tta (PONCHIELLI *La Gioconda*)
b[o]cca stretta (DONIZETTI *Don Pasquale*)

The word o means "either-or" and like the vocative is always closed.

Il mi[ɔ] bel f[o]ː[ɔ], [o] I[ɔ]ntan[ɔ], [o] vicin[ɔ] (MARCELLO "Song")
[O] n[ɔ]tte, [o] Dea (PICCINI "Song")
[O] mi[ɔ] Fernanc[ɔ] (DONIZETTI *La Favorita*)

Stressed o's in suffixes are always closed, as in nouns and adjectives ending in -ore, -oso, -osa, -ione.

Sm[ɔ]rfi[o]sa, malizi[o]sa (MOZART *Le Nozze di Figaro*)
Am[o]re mi[ɔ] (PUCCINI *Madama Butterfly*)
Maledizi[o]ne (VERDI *La Forza del Destino*)

The [u] *sound.* The Italian u is always long, as in the English word doom, but never diphthongized. Its pronunciation creates a difficulty for the English-speaking singer since the written u in English is pronounced like the IPA sounds U or ʌ. And even the oo (as in doom) is articulated further back in the mouth and is always somewhat diphthongized.

The Italian u is a pure vowel and is pronounced forward with rounded and protruded lips (protruded more than in pronouncing a closed o). The lips should be rounded into a pout, almost as if they were about to gently blow away some light object. It is important to impress on the singer the necessity of keeping mouth and throat relaxed as in a closed o position, otherwise the vowel will sound hooty or muffled. The tongue again should be kept low and the jaw be raised more than when pronouncing o. The u in Italian stays long whether it is an initial, medial, or final sound, and even before a double consonant. The grave accent likewise does not change the quality of the u.

Tutta la tua tribù (PUCCINI *Madama Butterfly*)
Omai tre voːte l'upupa (VERDI *Un Ballo in Maschera*)
Il tutor ricuserà (ROSSINI *Il Barbiere di Siviglia*)
Una gran nube turba il senno d'Otello (VERDI *Otello*)

All these examples contain the u as syllabic vowel. It can also be asyllabic or a semivowel.

L'aura che tu respiri (GLUCK "O del mio dolce ardor")
Questo o quella (VERDI *Rigoletto*)

SEMIVOWELS

The Italian language has two semivowels (or half vowels), which belong to the class of diphthongs.

1. The *i* can sometimes become a semivowel – expressed phonetically as [j] and pronounced exactly like the English *y* in *you*. In these combinations the [j] can stand before an a, ε, o, ɔ, and u sound. It is always a semivowel in its initial form when followed by another vowel as in [jɛri] (with the exceptions of some words of Greek derivation where the *i* stands for the Greek digamma as in *iacinto*). *i* is a semivowel between two other vowels (*acciaio*), in words ending in -iera, -iere (*cavaliere*); in verbal forms ending in -iamo, -iate (*amiamoci, facciate*). In words derived from Latin, such as *dieci* (from *decem*), *chiaro, obietto*, the *i* also is pronounced as a semivowel.

Siate felici (VERDI *La Traviata*)
Datemi vostri fiori (MOZART *Le Nozze di Figaro*)
Diedi i gioielli alla madonna al manto (PUCCINI *Tosca*)
Al *fiume* (VERDI *Rigoletto*)

An e following a [j] is always pronounced [ε].

2. The *u* can also at times become a semivowel – expressed phonetically as [w] – and is pronounced exactly as in the English *suave, persuasion*. The u becomes a semivowel in combination with q, g, and ng and can thus be found before a, e, i, ɔ. An o following a [w] is always pronounced [ɔ].

[Twɔna] (VERDI *Rigoletto*)
Quant' anni avete (PUCCINI *Madama Butterfly*)
Questo *uomo* fido provederà (PUCCINI *Tosca*)
Guidatemi all' ara (VERDI *Il Trovatore*)
Guerra, Guerra (VERDI *Aida*)
Sangue, sangue (VERDI *Otello*)

In all these the accent does not fall on the semivowel but on the preceding or following vowel. The following words have the accent on the i or the u and are therefore not considered semivowels: mío, mía, míe and all nouns with the endings, -io, -ia, and -ie, with the *i* stressed as in zío, Dío, allegría, osteríe. The separation between the two vowels is called hiatus. This rule is most important for the English-speaking singer who tends to put the ac-

[18]

cent on the wrong vowel (mió, miá, etc.). Other vowel combinations which do not contain semivowels due to the accentuated i's and u's are: túo, súo, túa, súa, túe, súe, dúe, búe, túi, súi, lúi, cúi, etc.

Musically, the distinction between vowel and semi-vowel must be very carefully made. Usually the semivow-el is expressed by one note only. The note must be divided in such a way that the stressed vowel gets the longer musical value. Figure 21 shows pure vowels of two syllables, and Figure 22 shows monosyllabic semi-vowels.

Figure 21. Pure vowels of two syllables

Figure 22. Semivowels of one syllable

Italian composers are usually conscious of these pure vowel and semivowel combinations and write their mu-

sic accordingly, as for instance Puccini in *La Bohème* (Fig. 23). Sometimes, in order to achieve a special effect,

Figure 23. Puccini, *La Bohème*

composers consciously change the rules of pronunci-ation. A famous example appears in Verdi's *Otello* (Fig. 24) where he changes the semivowel in paziente into a pure vowel to emphasize the slow, undermining, sugges-tive power of Iago over Otello. Similarly, in the fourth

Figure 24. Verdi, *Otello*

act of *La Traviata*, Verdi treats the word re-li-gi-o-ne as a five-syllable word, stressing thus Violetta's debility. In Desdemona's "Willow Song," he notates as shown in Figure 25. The stress lies on the e, which must there-fore be held longer than the a. The right way of separa-tion is therefore as shown in Figure 26. In the next line, oe, oi, ua, ue, ui, uo. These diphthongs are produced by pronouncing each vowel clearly and separately, without tying them together but without a y sound as in English (li-eto, not li-yeto). This is a frequent error and has to be corrected by accompanists and coaches.

Diphthongs in Italian are either vocalic (syllabic vowel plus asyllabic vowel), or semivocalic (semivowel plus syllabic vowel). If the semivowel precedes the syllabic vowel we speak of an ascending diphthong with the accent on the vowel as in words with ia, ie, [iɛ], io, iu, ua, [uɛ], ue, ui, uo, [uɔ]; otherwise the diphthong is called descending. The accent always stays on the vowel (ai, ei, [ɛi], oi, [ɔi], au, eu, [ɛu]).

Figure 28. Ways of singing diphthongs

Figure 25. Verdi, *Otello*

Figure 26. Verdi, *Otello*

Figure 27. Verdi, *Otello*

the vowels e and a and a fall on one short note and may therefore be divided equally as shown in Figure 27. Puccini separates i and a in the word nuziàl (Il nido nuziàl dov'è), (*Madama Butterfly*).

DIPHTHONGS

We speak of a diphthong if two vowels appear contiguously in the same syllable. The following vowel combinations are diphthongs if they belong to the same syllable: ae, ai, ao, au, ea, ei, eo, eu, ia, ie, io, iu, oa,

Of the two vowels of a diphthong, one or the other is accented. The musical accent must conform to the phonetic stress. The accented value gets the longest part of the note under which it stands. If the musical note above a diphthong is very short or the tempo very fast,

[20]

it is to be divided into equal parts. (See Fig. 28.) Similar diphthongs appearing in musical literature are aere, aiuto, lieto.

TRIPHTHONGS

Triphthongs are three contiguous vowels in one syllable. Each of these vowels must be pronounced clearly and separately, connected, however, by a legato. The musical accent must conform to the phonetic stress. The accentuated vowel gets the longest part of the note under which it stands. Triphthongs are formed by the vowel combinations aio, iei, iuo, uai, uia, uoi.

Miei cari, sedete (VERDI *La Traviata*)
Non ti conoscerà, se tu non vuoi (MOZART *Don Giovanni*)

CONSONANTS

The distinction between single and double consonants in Italian is very clear, more so than in any other language. I shall therefore treat them separately.

We have seen in the introductory remarks to this chapter that the consonants can be classified in several different ways. This book is written for accompanists and coaches, as an aid in their work with instrumental-

ists and vocalists. The chapter about phonetics concerns singers. For this reason, I shall classify the consonants by their degree of singability and shall start out with the voiced consonants, discussing the voiceless consonants afterwards.

The Italian pronounces his consonants just as he pronounces his vowels: clearly and definitely, with a distinct action of the speech apparatus. There is no delaying, no drawl, no muddiness as there sometimes is in English. Unless the vocal line requires some adjustment, the consonants are pronounced crisply, but without the explosive force that characterizes the consonants of some other languages.

Single consonants in Italian are – with the exception of some initial consonants with or without connection with final vowels of a preceding word – pronounced crisply but gently. The singer must not hesitate over them but must continue to the next vowel. No undue stress, no explosion must be added to the consonant. A consonant between two vowels must not interrupt the flow of vocal line.

Voiced consonants are singable to a greater or less degree. In Italian musical diction the voice does not linger on voiced consonants but proceeds to the next vowel, unless emotional, poetic, or onomatopoetic reasons demand a longer pause on the particular consonant.

The m sound. Phonetically, the m is a bilabial nasal sound (produced by both lips, with air escaping through the nose). The lips close firmly but without pressure. Standing by itself, a sung [m] amounts to a hum, since no tone can emerge from the mouth. A hum is usually sung piano but can be increased to a modest mezzo forte. Great care must be taken to arch the velum highly, to give more resonance to the hum. Otherwise, the nasal quality would be increased, as is sometimes necessary in French. An example is found in the Humming Chorus from Puccini's *Madama Butterfly* (Fig. 29).

Figure 29. Puccini, *Madama Butterfly,*
Humming Chorus

In some bel canto phrases where it is essential that the flow of vocal line from vowel to vowel must not be interrupted, the m should be pronounced weakly, the

lips not closing tightly. On such rather rare occasions, clarity of diction must be sacrificed for uninterrupted beauty of sound. These exceptions will occur more often in operas than in oratorios or songs (Fig. 30, 31).

Figure 30. Puccini, *La Bohème*

Figure 31. Mozart, *Don Giovanni*

The m between two vowels receives soft stress (amo). The m before or after a consonant receives moderate stress (tempo, calmo).

A*m*arilli, *m*ia bella (CACCINI "Madrigal Amarilli")
Caro *m*io ben, credi*m*i al*m*en (GIORDANI "Arietta")
Selve a*m*iche, o*m*brose piante (CALDARA "Arietta")

An initial m after a one-syllable word ending in a stressed vowel is pronounced like mm.

a *mm*e il ferro (VERDI *Don Carlo*)

[22]

e par che tenti riscattarlo da mme (MOZART *Le Nozze di Figaro*)

Similarly, the m of Maria between vowels in a phrase receives strong stress.

Ave Mmaria (VERDI *Otello*)
Gesùmmaria (LEONCAVALLO *Pagliacci*)

The n sound. The n is an alveolar nasal sound, produced by flattening the most forward part of the tongue against the upper alveolar ridge, with the tip of the tongue touching the upper teeth. At the same time the soft palate should be in a raised position to avoid too much nasal sound. Initial n's and n's between two vowels must be produced this way, but care should be taken not to exaggerate the pressure of the tongue and not to explode the n by a too sudden release of the tongue.

The n is soft between two vowels (lana), and moderate before or after another vowel (mente, Arno).

Tu menti (PUCCINI *Madama Butterfly*)
Enzo adorato (PONCHIELLI *La Gioconda*)
Cruda, funesta smania (DONIZETTI *Lucia di Lammermoor*)
Pronto a far tutto la notte e il giorno, sempre d'intorno (ROSSINI *Il Barbiere di Siviglia*)

Initial n gets added stress. Final n gets moderate stress.

Tre giorni son che Nina (PERGOLESI "Nina")
Il balen del suo sorriso (VERDI *Il Trovatore*)

Again, great care should be taken not to lower the velum too much. This would decrease the size of the resonance cavity of the mouth and increase the nasality of the n.

The n changes its quality when followed by an f or v. It then assumes a slightly nasal sound. If followed by g or k, the n becomes [ŋ]. If preceded by a g, the combination becomes [ɲ].

The ng [ŋ] sound. The alveolar n followed by a g or k becomes a new velar sound. It is produced by a meeting of the raised back of the tongue and the lowered soft palate (velum). There should be no pressure and the sound must be produced in the back of the mouth, *not* in the throat. It has a slight nasal quality which should not be overstressed by lowering the velum too much.

The n and the following g or k are not molded together as in the German jung, or the English sing. The tongue simply moves back from the alveolar to the velar position.

Fruga ogni angolo (PUCCINI *Tosca*)

Ingannata (PUCCINI *Tosca*)

There are no initial or final [ŋ]'s in Italian.

The gn sound. The gn ([ɲ] phonetically) belongs to the n group, although spelled gn in Italian. It is a palatal nasal sound, and is sometimes called a liquid consonant. It is produced by flattening the middle part of the tongue against the hard palate, while the tip of the tongue is anchored against the lower teeth. The uvula is down. In Spanish, the spelling for [ɲ] is ñ, in Portuguese nh. It has no equivalent in English or German. The French spelling is the same as the Italian wherever it appears.

The nearest sound in English would be the ny as, for instance, in canyon.

In Italian, the [ɲ] can stand before any of the seven vowel sounds.

O*gni* città, o*gni* paese (MOZART *Don Giovanni*)
Il feritore? I*gn*oto (GIORDANO *Andrea Chenier*)
Ma, *gn*affe a me, non se la fa (VERDI *La Forza del Destino*)

The stress of the [ɲ] is moderate in the initial position (*gnocchi*), but strong in the middle of a word (*ignoto*).

The l sound. The l is a dental-alveolar voiced consonant, produced by placing the most forward part of the tongue against the upper teeth near the gum ridge. This l is, therefore, produced forward, the breath escaping along the sides of the tongue. It is of the greatest importance that English-speaking singers are taught how to produce a forward l, since they habitually tend to produce the l further back in a more guttural way. This is not good for a forward voice production. After the dental-alveolar placement, the tongue should come down rapidly to the region of the lower teeth in order to form the following vowel, or should proceed to the position of the next consonant, if the l is followed by such a sound. The l can be given different grades of stress. It is soft between two vowels and moderate before or after a consonant.

Non è su *l*ei, ne*l* suo fragile petto (VERDI *Un Ballo in Maschera*)
Il balen del suo sorriso (VERDI *Il Trovatore*)

In the words là and lì, the l receives strong stress.

The initial l is produced so easily that almost all languages use it for illustrating melodies and rhythms, usually followed by an a. In sustained, melodic singing the stress on the l is soft. When expressing rhythmical patterns, the stress on the l becomes moderate or even strong, approximating ll (Fig. 32).

lo, lo-lo-le-ra - lo, lo-lo-le-ra - la!

Figure 32. Mozart, Don Giovanni

The gl sound. The [ʎ] belongs to the l group, though spelled gl in Italian. It is a palatal-alveolar sound produced initially like the l, but with the center of the tongue pressed against the hard palate. The sides of the tongue are not so free as they are in pronouncing l, and the air passage is thus narrowed along the side of the tongue. In Spanish, [ʎ] is expressed by ll (Sevi*ll*a), in Portuguese by lh (ore*lh*a). French and German do not have the [ʎ] sound, except in foreign names. Not all sounds spelled gl in Italian are [ʎ]'s. Initial and medial gl's are always in the g class, unless they are followed by i.

Gloria all' Egitto, ad Iside (VERDI Aïda)

l' egloghe dei pastori (GIORDANO Andrea Chenier)

But: Nella bionda egli ha l' usanza (MOZART Don Giovanni)

The [ʎ] before i gets moderate stress.

Ecco i fogli (VERDI La Forza del Destino)

The [ʎ] before i followed by a, e, o, or u gets strong stress.

Lo vedremo, veglio audace (VERDI Ernani)
Voglio piena libertà (PUCCINI La Bohème)
Quest' uomo ha moglie e sconcie voglie ha nel cor (PUCCINI La Bohème)

Some initial and medial *gli* combinations, derived mostly from foreign words, do not take the [ʎ] sound, as in *gli*cerina, gero*gli*fico, and negl*igente* and in combinations with n (An*gl*ia).

e sopra tutto questo al mio braccio impresso geroglifico (MOZART Le Nozze di Figaro)

The v sound. The v is a voiced labiodental fricative sound, produced by putting the upper teeth lightly and loosely against the inside part of the lower lip. The tongue should again be in a low position but should be relaxed, without touching the lower teeth. Thus a narrow opening is effected through which the sound emerges. The v must always be voiced (it must vibrate a little).

The English-speaking singer is prone to neglect the v by failing to bring the lower lip and upper teeth into contact. This should be corrected by the accompanist or coach. The v is stressed softly between two vowels, moderately before or after a consonant.

amò tanto la vita (PUCCINI *Tosca*)
Ernani, involami (VERDI *Ernani*)

In some phrases, as in sù via, ho visto, dove vai, e venti, the v receives strong stress (suvvia, ho vvisto).

Suvvia, spicciatevi (LEONCAVALLO *Pagliacci*)
Non ho visto compar Alfio (MASCAGNI *Cavalleria Rusticana*)

Initial v is stressed strongly in some cases if emphasis is to be given to the word.

è vile, vile (GIORDANO *Andrea Chenier*)

The voiced s sound. This voiced consonant is sometimes expressed by s, sometimes by [z]. It is an alveolar-dental fricative sound produced forward by cradling the tongue upwards, its tip almost (but not actually) touching the center of the upper front teeth. This sound should always be pronounced in a relaxed manner, never hurried. It is equivalent to the s sound in the English word has.

The z in Italian is pronounced in different ways, according to geographical situation. The northern parts generally pronounce it [z]. Tuscany mixes the pronunciation so that it sometimes sounds s, sometimes [z]; the rest of Italy changes the voiced [z] into a voiceless, though softly stressed, s. No over-all pronunciation rule exists. In singing it will be best always to voice the s when the s stands between two vowels or before another voiced consonant, such as b, d, g, l, m, n, r, or v.

Guidatemi al ridicolo oltraggio d'un rasoio (PUCCINI *La Bohème*)

Sbarazzate all' l'istante (PUCCINI *Madama Butterfly*)
Una smania, un pizzicare (ROSSINI *Il Barbiere di Siviglia*)
Sgomento io non ho (PUCCINI *Tosca*)

The stress is always soft, only very slightly less so before another voiced consonant.

s between two vowels of which the first one belongs

to a prefix is treated like an initial s, which is always voiceless. Likewise, the reflexive pronoun si, used as a suffix, has a voiceless s.

Qui nel cor mi risuonò (ROSSINI *Il Barbiere di Siviglia*)
Ogni sagezza chiudesi (VERDI *Rigoletto*)

The b sound. The b is a voiced bilabial occlusive sound. This means that the lips must be closed lightly, remain in this position for a split second — but long enough to effect an occlusion, and open to let the air emerge. The lip muscles must not be tightened.

In Italian singing diction the occlusion must always be light. In all occlusive sounds, voiced or voiceless, preserving the melodic line may force the singer not to effect complete occlusion — in other words, to fake the occlusion. It is up to the accompanist or coach to decide when this should be done.

The b should never be exploded, as it sometimes is in German. It receives soft stress between two vowels and before a consonant, moderate stress after a consonant.

La donna è mobile (VERDI *Rigoletto*)

Dammi un bacio, o non fai niente (MOZART *Le Nozze di Figaro*)
Ed assoporo allor la bramosia sottil (PUCCINI *La Bohème*)
O dolce viso di mite circonfuso alba lunar (PUCCINI *La Bohème*)

In exclamations, the b can be strongly stressed.

Che bbella bambina (PUCCINI *La Bohème*)

The d sound. The d is a voiced dental occlusive sound. The tip of the tongue touches the point where the upper teeth ridge and the hard palate meet. After remaining there for a split second to effect occlusion, the tongue moves on to the next sound suddenly but lightly, with the emergence of some air.

The d between two vowels and before another consonant is stressed softly; it receives moderate stress after another consonant.

Ah, non credea mirarti (BELLINI *La Sonnambula*)
Ah, Padre mio (VERDI *Rigoletto*)
Come, m'ardon le ciglia (VERDI *Otello*)

The d of Dio between two vowels in a phrase receives strong stress.

Ah! Dio! (PUCCINI *Tosca*)

The [dz] (z) sound. The z sound expressed phonetically by [dz] can also be voiceless and is, in that case, represented phonetically as [ts].

The [dz] is a voiced dental semiocclusive sound. Its production starts in the same way as the production of the d and is continued by the sides of the tongue touching the alveolar ridge. In this way air can escape through a narrow passage which explains the classification of the [dz] as semiocclusive. The production is fast, and there should be no hissing; [dz] is a gentle sound.

There is no hard and fast rule to determine when the Italian z is voiced [dz] and when it is voiceless [ts]. Regional differences exist. A good orthophonetic dictionary will have to be consulted in case of doubt.

To students of linguistics I should add that the [dz] usually derives from the Latin voiced d (mediu → mediu dzo) or from the Greek zeta (as in the Italian dzona). The Latin voiceless t usually changes into an Italian [ts] (martiu → marzo).

An initial z may be voiced as in zero, zara. Likewise, a voiced z can stand between two vowels as in ozono, or it can come after another consonant, as in garza. Even zz can be voiced, as in all verbal suffixes on -izzare, or in words like olezzo. The stress on the initial [dz] and [dz] following another consonant is moderate; [dz] between two vowels gets a strong stress (lo ddzero, Donid-dzetti).

Che soave zefiretto (MOZART *Le Nozze di Figaro*)
Ei gongolava arzillo, pettoruto (PUCCINI *La Bohème*)
Per tener ben fuori le zanzare, i parenti (PUCCINI *Madama Butterfly*)

The g sound. The g and gh consonant in Italian is a voiced velar occlusive sound produced by the contact of the soft palate with the back part of the tongue. This causes a split second of occlusion which has to be resolved smoothly and without explosion. The tip of the tongue should be anchored against the lower teeth. The accompanist or coach should see to it that the meeting point of tongue and soft palate (velum) is not so far back as to make the g sound guttural.

g in Italian may be pronounced [g] (gone) or [dz] (Joe). It is pronounced [g] before the vowels a, o, and u. It adds the silent h to keep its sound before e and i (ghe, ghi). It is also pronounced [g] before an r and sometimes before an l, as I have said when discussing the gl sound. g and gh have a soft stress between two vowels and before another consonant, and a moderate stress after another vowel.

Un' agonia (PONCHIELLI *La Gioconda*)
Ogni borgo, ogni paese (MOZART *Don Giovanni*)
Scrivo ancor tre righe a volo (PUCCINI *La Bohème*)
Ora sono di ghiaccio (MOZART *Le Nozze di Figaro*)

The [dʒ] sound. ge or gi ([dʒ]) is a voiced alveolar-palatal semiocclusive sound (as in the English *job*), actually a combination of d and [ʒ] sounds. The tongue takes its position at the alveolar ridge and its center touches the hard palate. The sound which results leaves a small space for the breath to escape. The [dʒ] must be pronounced gently to preserve its full voiced quality. The [dʒ] is expressed in Italian by the letter g in front of an e or i. If the same sound is desired before an a, o, or u, a mute i must be inserted (as in giardino, gioia, giù).

The stress on the [dʒ] is soft between two vowels,
L'agile mandola nè accompagna il suon (VERDI *Otello*)

Io gelo (VERDI *Il Trovatore*)
gira la cote, gira, gira (PUCCINI *Turandot*)
Dunque in giardin verrai (MOZART *Le Nozze di Figaro*)
O gioia (VERDI *Rigoletto*)

moderate after another consonant.

Urge l'opra (PUCCINI *Tosca*)

The j sound. The [j] can sometimes still be found in old Italian scores or books. It is now replaced entirely by i and is either a vowel or semivowel.

che tai baje costan poco (VERDI *Rigoletto*)

The r sound. The r, because of the various ways in which it can be produced, has a special position in the Italian consonants. In its pure Italian form, it is a voiced alveolar vibrant produced by keeping the tongue forward with the tip against the upper alveolar ridge, and vibrating it by a flutter or roll which, depending on the stress, is repeated from one to four times. The breath escapes over the tongue, not along its sides. The r is sometimes called dental r, sometimes rolled r. It is used by most Italians and is easy for the English-speaking singer to master. The roll of the r must not be overdone. Some

Italian singers use the uvular (or guttural) r which is rolled or fluttered against the back of the tongue. It is very difficult to change a student's manner of producing the r, but since the English (though not the American) way is similar to the Italian way, the accompanist or coach should have no difficulties with it. The stress on the r, on the other hand, creates difficulties for the English-speaking singer.

r between two vowels always receives soft stress — one flutter is enough.

Initial and final r and r before and after another consonant are pronounced with moderate to strong stress, mostly the latter. From two to four flutters will be necessary. Italian ears are very sensitive to the pronunciation of the r; a strong r between vowels repels them. The following are examples of soft stress.

O mio amore (PUCCINI *Tosca*)
Molto raro complimento (PUCCINI *Madama Butterfly*)

Examples of moderate stress are as follows.

All' armi (VERDI *Il Trovatore*)
In dietro (ROSSINI *Il Barbiere di Siviglia*)

Ah frate, frate! (VERDI *La Forza del Destino*)

The r fulfills another important vocal function. The trill or flutter enables the singer to shift from one vocal position to another without disturbing the phrase. Such r's act like the neutral gear on a car: it is easy to shift into any position from there.

VOICELESS CONSONANTS

Voiceless consonants contain no trace of singability. In Italian lyric diction the voice does not linger on them but, having sung the preceding vowel, ties the consonant, or group of consonants, to the next vowel.

In Italian, voiceless consonants are never aspirated, as in German or English, unless emotional, poetical, or onomatopoetical reasons require it. In operatic singing, where strong projection is more important than in concert singing, some initial voiceless consonants — mostly f, p, and k — must receive strong stress in order to be heard. English-speaking singers must be constantly reminded of this, because they frequently neglect strong stress on these initial sounds.

The f sound. The f is a voiceless labiodental fricative

[30]

sound. It is produced like its voiced counterpart (see p. 24). However, the upper teeth and the inside of the lower lip come together with more firmness. The small amount of air must emerge more suddenly, but without an explosion.

The stress on the f is soft between two vowels, and if it precedes another consonant, moderate if it follows another consonant.

Urna fatale del mio destino (VERDI *La Forza del Destino*)
O mio Rodolfo (PUCCINI *La Bohème*)
Ninfe! Elfi! Silfi! (VERDI *Falstaff*)

Initial f without a preceding vowel in the same word should, as I said before, be stressed strongly in operatic singing.

Finch'han dal vino (MOZART *Don Giovanni*)
Credo con fermio cuor (VERDI *Otello*)

The f also receives strong stress after exclamations like ah, oh, o, and deh.

Ah frate, frate! (VERDI *La Forza del Destino*)

The s sound. The s is a voiceless dental-alveolar fricative sound. It is produced exactly as its voiced counter-part (see p. 26) except that the voiceless s is produced by letting out the stream of air suddenly, although with less explosion than a German or English voiceless s.

The initial s in Italian is voiceless before a vowel and before a voiceless consonant.

Il dolce suono (DONIZETTI *Lucia di Lammermoor*)
Il suo stemma (PUCCINI *Tosca*)
A te la spada io rendo (VERDI *Don Carlo*)
Sfogati, amazzami (MOZART *Don Giovanni*)

s in the middle of a word is voiceless before a voiceless consonant and following any consonant.

Entrando per gli occhi, mi fe' sospirar (LEGRENZI "Che Fiero Costume")
Tal pensiero perchè conturba ognor (VERDI *Rigoletto*)

The s receives medium stress at the beginning of a word and before and after consonants.

Like the z, s does not conform to an over-all rule of pronunciation. It varies according to geographical situations. Mese is pronounced [meze] in northern Italy; in Tuscany the pronunciation varies between [meze] and [mese] according to local differences; southern Italy almost always pronounces it [mese] (with soft stress). It may be said, however, that modern diction tends to make the s between vowels voiceless, for instance in some root endings on -es and -os as in geloso, mese, spese. But such words as paese and cortese, on the other hand, have the voiced [z].

The words casa, cosa, chiuso, and naso are also usually voiceless, but with very soft stress; otherwise they would sound like cassa, cossa, and so on. Until Italian phoneticists decide on an over-all rule for pronunciation of the s, the accompanist and coach will do well to ignore the regional variations and teach the above rules to their singers:

s between two vowels is voiceless and receives moderate stress in the case of word combinations like offriasi, chiudesi that stand for si offria, si chiude.

The p sound. The p is a voiceless bilabial occlusive sound. It is produced like the b (see p. 27) but with greater occlusion of the lips. For the operatic singing of initial occlusive voiceless sounds (p, t, k) I advocate slight explosion, since these sounds are sorely neglected by English-speaking singers and get lost in our opera houses and concert halls. They should, however, have a less explosive sound than their German counterparts. The pressure of the lips in forming the p must be firm, no breath should be allowed to escape.

The initial p receives a strong stress, the p between two vowels and before a consonant is stressed softly, p after a consonant receives moderate stress.

O *p*atria mia (VERDI *Aïda*)
A*p*erta! Arcangeli! (PUCCINI *Tosca*)
A*p*rite! A*p*rite! (VERDI *Otello*)
Em*p*ia razza (VERDI *Aïda*)

Some initial p's in phrasal connections are strongly stressed.

Fra *pp*oco alla meco verrà (MOZART *Le Nozze di Figaro*)
E *pp*oi? E *pp*oi? (VERDI *Otello*)

The t sound. The t is a voiceless dental occlusive sound, produced like the voiced d (see p. 27) except that the removal of the occlusion by the tongue has to be effected with more energy, less softness. The t must never be aspirated, like the German t, but a slight explosion of initial t's is recommended to insure clear diction and projection.

[32]

The initial t and the t after a consonant receive moderate stress; t between two vowels and before a consonant is stressed softly.

O terra addio (VERDI *Aïda*)
Vissi d'arte (PUCCINI *Tosca*)
E Silva non ritorna (VERDI *Ernani*)
Scorsa fu la notte al tripudio (DONIZETTI *Lucia di Lammermoor*)

Some initial t's in phrasal connections receive strong stress, as in sò ttutto, così ttardi.

The [ts] (z) *sound.* This [ts] sound is a combination of the voiceless t and s sounds. It is expressed by the letter z, which in Italian can also be voiced and is, in that case, phonetically represented by [dz].

The [ts] is a voiceless, dental, semiocclusive sound. It starts the same way as the t, but the tongue cannot come down to a relaxed s position. The sides of the tongue touch the upper gum ridge, thus allowing the air to escape through a narrow passage. This is the reason why the [ts] is called semiocclusive. No hissing must occur in the pronunciation of the [ts].

As we said when discussing the [dz], no over-all rule exists concerning whether a z is pronounced voiced or voiceless. A good orthophonetic dictionary must be consulted in each case.

An initial z may be voiceless as in [ts]itto, [ts]io. z between vowels may be voiceless as in vi[ts]io, a[ts]ione, [ets]io. Likewise, z may be voiceless after consonants, as in sen[ts]a, Fin[ts]a, an[ts]i, al[ts]ati. The stress varies greatly. [ts] between vowels can be stressed strongly, whereas it receives moderate stress after another consonant.

Alzati! là tuo figlio a te concedo riveder (VERDI *Un Ballo in Maschera*)
La mia candida veste nuziale (VERDI *Otello*)

The [k] (c, ch) *sound.* The c and ch sounds expressed phonetically by [k] are voiceless, velar, occlusive sounds, produced like their voiced counterpart, the [g] (see p. 28) except that the contact between tongue and soft palate must be sudden and more firm. No aspiration is permissible and the resulting slight explosion should not be overdone, except on initial [k]'s for reasons of clarity.

The Italian c is pronounced [k] if it stands before a, o, or u. Before an e or i, a silent h is added to effect the same pronunciation, [k]. c before another consonant (l, r) is also pronounced [k].

[k] is stressed softly between two vowels, and before an r or l; moderately after another consonant.

Caro mio ben (GIORDANI "Caro Mio Ben")
Chi va là (MOZART Don Giovanni)
Che fai (PUCCINI Tosca)
Come va l'eco della pia campana (CATALANI La Wally)
Ell' è una mia cugina (MOZART Le Nozze di Figaro)
Perchè me ne rimuneri così (PUCCINI Tosca)
Mi chiamano Mimi (PUCCINI La Bohème)
È scritto (VERDI La Forza del Destino)

In some phrasal combinations the [k] receives reinforced stress, as in qualche ccosa.

The [kw] (qu) sound. The consonant q in Italian appears only in combination with the vowel u and is expressed, phonetically, by the symbol [kw]. The pronunciation corresponds exactly to the pronunciation of the Italian cu.

Questo o quella (VERDI Rigoletto)
Quand' ero paggio (VERDI Falstaff)
Iniquo (VERDI Rigoletto)
Per offrirvi l' acqua benedetta (PUCCINI Tosca)

The stress is soft between two vowels, moderate after another consonant.

The [ks] (x) sound. The x is a combination of voiceless k and s sounds. In Italian, it appears only in foreign words, as in Xidias. Usually the x is supplanted by z, s, or ss.

The [tʃ] sound. The [tʃ] sound is a voiceless alveolar-palatal semiocclusive sound, corresponding to the ch in the English words church, fetch. Its production is the same as for voiced [dʒ] (see p. 29) except that the occlusion and subsequent release have to be somewhat firmer. But there must be no explosion. The [tʃ] sound in Italian is as gentle as its voiceless quality will allow. [tʃ] is pronounced when a c stands in front of an e or i. If the same sound is desired before an a, o, or u, a silent i has to be interpolated (cia, cio, ciu).

[tʃ] receives soft stress between two vowels, moderate stress after another consonant.

Ha ciascun i suoi gusti (MOZART Le Nozze di Figaro)
Burro e cacio (PUCCINI La Bohème)
Pace, pace (VERDI La Forza del Destino)
Scuoti quella fronda di ciliegio (PUCCINI Madama Butterfly)

La c*i*urma, ovè (PONCHIELLI *La Gioconda*)

Sometimes a mute i is also put between a c and an e, as in cieca or cielo. The pronunciation is the same as if it were spelled ce.

Cielo e mar (PONCHIELLI *La Gioconda*)

The [ʃ] *sound.* The [ʃ] sound corresponds to the English sh. It is a voiceless alveolar-palatal fricative sound and not a combination of consonants. It is produced by the upward-curled tip of the tongue which approaches the hard palate, well back of the upper gum ridge. At the same time, the side edges of the tongue should be anchored against the upper molars and the lips should be rounded but motionless. After this procedure the air stream is gently exploded. [ʃ] is spelled sc before an e and i, and sci before a, o, and u. It is stressed moderately after a consonant and strongly between two vowels and as the initial sound of a word.

Non fate sc*e*ne qui (PUCCINI *La Bohème*)
Brutto sc*i*miotto (ROSSINI *Il Barbiere di Siviglia*)
Sc*i*agurato! Così del mio cor gioco ti prendi (MOZART *Don Giovanni*)
Siamo all' asc*i*utto (PUCCINI *La Bohème*)

A mute i is sometimes interjected between [ʃ] and e, as in scienza (although this word, if spelled scïenza, ought to be pronounced [ʃi-en-tsa). Otherwise the pronunciation of these words is identical with sce.

The [sk] *sound.* sc before an a, o, and u is pronounced [sk]. If the same pronunciation is desired before an e or i, an h must be interjected before the vowel (sch).

Come sc*o*glio (MOZART *Così fan tutte*)
Ti crucci d'uno sc*a*cco (PUCCINI *Manon Lescaut*)
Tu dormi in sc*u*deria (VERDI *Rigoletto*)
La *sch*iena oggi vi prude (LEONCAVALLO *Pagliacci*)
È *sch*erzo, è follia (VERDI *Un Ballo in Maschera*)

The h *sound.* The h in Italian is *always* silent be it at the beginning of a word, in its middle, or at the end, as in ho, hanno, chi, paghi, oh, deh.

Fame non *h*o (PUCCINI *Tosca*)
Ch' *h*ai di nuovo, buffon (VERDI *Rigoletto*)

DOUBLE CONSONANTS

The difference between single and double consonants in Italian is most important. A single consonant is always pronounced gently, with different degrees of stress — soft, moderate, and only sometimes strong. Double consonants are always stressed strongly. Distinctive pronunciation of a double consonant is the only way to mark the difference between similarly spelled words: eco-ecco, caro-carro, fato-fatto, rida-ridda, casa-cassa, pala-palla, nono-nonno, fumo-fummo, quadro-soqquadro, regia-reggia, papa-pappa, libra-libbra, tufo-tuffo, lego-leggo.

Voiced double consonants are ll, mm, nn, rr, gg ([ddʒ]), bb, dd, gg, zz ([ddz]), ggh, vv; voiceless: cc ([ttʃ]) or cch ([kk]), ff, pp, ss, tt, cqu, or qqu ([kkw]).

Double consonants are pronounced like one prolonged consonant and are not divided into two consonants. Double consonants in Italian shorten the preceding vowel but do not necessarily open closed vowels as they do in German.

CLOSED VOWELS: Povero Rigoletto (VERDI *Rigoletto*) Sei buona, o mia Musetta (PUCCINI *La Bohème*)

OPEN VOWELS: Attendi frat[ɛ]llo (VERDI *Rigoletto*)

The voiced double consonants can fulfill an important vocal function. They can carry the vocal line from vowel to vowel. Double consonants give more intensity, impetus, and importance to the words that contain them. While all double consonants are being drawn to the succeeding tone, the voiced consonant ought to receive some portion of singing sound. This holds true especially for the ll, mm, nn, rr, and vv sounds (Figs. 33, 34).

Do - nne ve - de - te

Figure 33. Mozart, Le Nozze di Figaro

con eleganza

Questa o que - lla ___ per me pa-ri so - no

Figure 34. Verdi, Rigoletto

The occlusive and semiocclusive double consonants, voiced and voiceless — bb, dd, gg, pp, tt, cc ([kk]), zz ([tts]), and [ddz], qqu ([kkw]), cc ([ttʃ]), gg ([ddʒ]) — are produced in the following way: the tongue and lips form the double consonant at the end of the preceding tone, *but without pronouncing it.* After a split second, air is exploded gently and the occlusion is ended while the speech apparatus slides over to the succeeding vowel. A minute interruption of the vocal line thus is inevitable but serves to stress the double consonant (Figs. 35–38).

Figure 35. Verdi, *Aida*

Figure 36. Verdi, *Il Trovatore*

Figure 37. Puccini, *La Bohème*

Figure 38. Puccini, *La Bohème*

There is only one example of a qqu (double consonant with following ser ivowel) in the Italian language. It appears in the word soqquadro (Fig. 39).

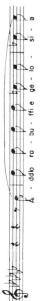

Figure 39. Verdi, *La Forza del destino*, an example of the only qq in Italian

Some Italian words end in l, m, n, and r. If these final consonants are followed by words beginning with the same consonan: they will sound like double consonants and should be treated as such.

Or lasciami al lavoro (PUCCINI *Tosca*)
Andiam maestro (BOITO *Mefistofele*)
Disperda il ciel [ʌ]i affanni (VERDI *Otello*)
Vile son nato (VERDI *Otello*)
Per ridurre un geloso allo sbaraglio (PUCCINI *Tosca*)

COMBINATIONS OF CONSONANTS

Combinaticns of consonants exist in Italian, although it has fewer than any other language. They do not present insurmountable difficulties for the English-speaking singer. Some combinations may be initial, as in words beginning with bl, br, cl, cr; some in combinations of three consonants, as in words starting with sbl, sbr, scl, scr, sdr, sfr, sgr, spl, spr. Other combinations — as in bbl, bbr, ccl, ccr, ddr, ffl, ffr — can be found only in the middle of a word. There may also be combinations of final consonants (l, m, n, r) with initial ones: mc, mgl, ngl, nm, rgl, and others.

In all these combinations of consonants the musical sound falls on the preceding vowel and the combination of consonants is drawn to the next vowel, which receives the next musical sound. Since only a minimum amount of time should be lost in pronouncing the consonant combination in order not to interrupt the vocal line, the accompanist or coach must impress upon the singer the necessity of enunciating these consonant combinations lightly and rapidly.

LIAISON AND SEPARATION

The great majority of Italian words end in vowels. Many words start with vowels. In singing, these final and initial vowels must be connected by liaison. The rules of the liaisons of different vowels are most important and must be completely understood by the accompanist or coach. Musically, these vowel connections are usually expressed by only one note. The reason for this is that the Italian language normally connects vowels, and any Italian does it naturally.

I have shown how to sing diphthongs and triphthongs. Connected vowels are sung very similarly. The stressed vowel gets the greater part of the value of the musical note, the unstressed vowel has to be content with a smaller part.

LIAISONS OF IDENTICAL VOWELS

If two words are connected by final and initial vowels, identical in print if not in sound, the liaison will simply have the effect of a prolonged vowel sound. If the phonetic values of these two vowels are different (one short, one long) the resulting liaison has the sound of the long vowel.

Bell*a a*dorata (VERDI *Don Carlo*)
E sent*o i*l fang*o o*rdinario in me (VERDI *Otello*)
Nobili sens*i i*n vero (VERDI *La Traviata*)

[38]

In evaluating the length that each vowel receives in combinations of different vowels, one will have to take several elements into consideration. Firstly, if one of the two or more vowels is long and closed, it will receive the greater share of the value of the note and the other vowel or vowels the lesser. Secondly, the length of the musical note will determine whether the longer vowel is prolonged. If the note is very short or the tempo very fast, the time value of the musical note becomes so minute that both vowels may receive the same amount of time. Thirdly, accentuated vowels receive a greater share of the available musical note, unstressed ones a smaller one. Unaccentuated i's before an a, [ɛ], [ɔ], or [ɔ] become half vowels. The vowel of an article is always shortened. The word è is always lengthened.

A few examples may suffice to illustrate these rules. It would be too ponderous to enumerate all possible combinations which serve as liaisons. Figure 40 shows liaisons of two sounds, Figure 41 liaisons of three.

Sometimes, although rarely, final and initial vowels should be separated. There are several reasons for this. First, punctuation sometimes forces a separation instead

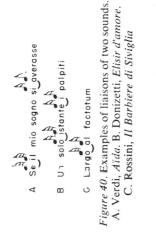

A Se il mio sogno si avverasse

B Un solo istante i palpiti

C Largo al factotum

Figure 40. Examples of liaisons of two sounds.
A. Verdi, *Aida.* B. Donizetti, *Elisir d'amore.*
C. Rossini, *Il Barbiere di Siviglia*

A Voi che sapete che cosa è amor

B Quando narravi l'esule tua vita'e i fieri eventi e i lunghi tuoi dolor

C e che nell'ira io nomo

D Che farò senza Euridice

Figure 41. Examples of liaisons of three sounds.
A. Mozart, *Le Nozze di Figaro.* B. Verdi, *Otello.*
C. Verdi, *Otello.* D. Gluck, *Orfeo ed Euridice*

of liaison. Generally the composer will write separate notes, but it may happen that he trusts to the understanding of coaches and singers, as in Figure 42. Here the comma as well as the phrasing make the change to the rendering shown in Figure 43 preferable. In Figure 44, the liaison must be interrupted, according to the logical declamation of the sentence and the e has to be separated from the o and tied to i.

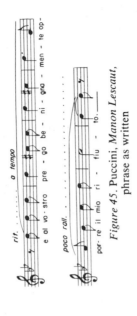

Figure 42. Puccini, *Madama Butterfly*, phrase as written

Figure 43. Puccini, *Madama Butterfly*, phrase as it should be sung

Figure 44. Puccini, *Tosca*

Secondly, for reasons of phrasing: if a musical phrase is too long, the singer must take a breath somewhere.

It may be that must happen where a liaison would otherwise be made (Fig. 45), but here the phrase is simply too long to be sung in one breath. The accompanist or coach is therefore justified in changing the phrase as shown in Figure 46.

Figure 45. Puccini, *Manon Lescaut*, phrase as written

Figure 46. Puccini, *Manon Lescaut*, phrase as it should be sung

Sometimes the separation (hiatus) is optional and depends on the singer's vocal abilities. Rodolfo's and Marcello's duet in Act 4 of *La Bohème* ends as shown in Figure 47. If the singers can muster a beautiful dimin-

uendo on the fermata tone, the vowels could be divided as shown in Figure 48. The breath should be an expression breath to portray the Bohemians' nostalgia and resignation – although not too much time should be lost in breathing. The fermata tone should be held very long, diminish, and end in the finest possible pianissimo. Some conductors, it must be said, frown upon such a change.

Rod.: poi - che è mor - to a - mor.
Mor.: e a - spet - ta il vil mio cuor.

Figure 47. Puccini, La Bohème, phrase as written

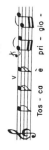

Rod.: poi - che è mor - to a - mor.
Mor.: e a - spet - ta il vil mio cuor.

Figure 48. Puccini, La Bohème, phrase as it might be sung

Thirdly, strong rhythmic or dramatic impetus may, in very rare cases, force the singer to separate final and initial vowels which would otherwise be connected (Fig. 49). Puccini asks that this be sung "with great

passion," drama so strong that the liaison would not do it justice. It is therefore proper to disconnect the two

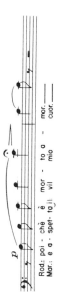

l'in - na - mc - ra - to _ To-sca è pri - gio - nie - ra. _

Figure 49. Puccini, Tosca, phrase as written

Tos - ca è pri - gio -

Figure 50. Puccini, Tosca, phrase as it should be sung

fio - ri, e l'oc-chio è un

Figure 51. Puccini, Manon Lescaut

vowels, divide the eighth note into two sixteenth notes, and breathe between (Fig. 50).

Fourth, in turns or other embellishments that are written on a liaison, the two vowels must be distributed according to natural diction (Fig. 51).

OMISSION AND DISTRIBUTION OF VOWELS

Omission and distribution of vowels are bad habits of teachers and singers. Since the connection of some vowels, especially at faster tempi, is difficult and demands special effort, many coaches simply tell their charges to omit some of the vowels. Such an omission does not conform to the composer's wishes and is almost always avoidable. The only time vowels may (but need not) be omitted is when the abbreviation does not change the meaning of the phrase. Otherwise, omitting vowels or distributing them among different musical notes should be avoided.

All vocal music contains melismas, meaning that more than one musical note is written over one syllable or one

Figure 52. A melisma

Figure 53. Same notes, sung on separate syllables

Figure 54. Mozart, *Don Giovanni,* passage as written

vowel. The notation for a melisma shows a connection between the musical notes (Fig. 52). If each note were to be sung on a separate syllable the notation would be as shown in Figure 53. Similarly, in the passage from

Figure 55. Mozart, *Don Giovanni,* passage as it should not be sung

Figure 56. Mozart, *Don Giovanni,* passage as written

Figure 57. Mozart, *Don Giovanni,* passage as it should not be sung

Figure 58. Mozart, *Don Giovanni,* passage as written

[42]

Don Giovanni shown in Figure 54, Mozart definitely wanted the liaison on bonded sung on the first of the two sixteenth notes; otherwise, he would have notated as shown in Figure 55. In the same aria, a few measures

Figure 59. Mozart, *Don Giovanni*, phrase from passage as it should not be sung

Figure 60. Mozart, *Don Giovanni*, phrase from passage as it should not be sung

later, Zerlina should sing the passage as shown in Figure 56, and not as shown in Figure 57. Still later, she should sing the passage as shown in Figure 58. Many singers, even in the best opera houses, sing phrases from this as shown in Figures 59 and 60. There is not the slightest need for such a change. It simply loses Mozart's melismatic pattern of two connected and one separate eighth note in one place and of one separate and two connected eighths in the other place. Examples of this

kind of wrong distribution can be found in performances of almost any composer's work, but the offense against Mozart is possibly the worst.

One more example: Puccini, in the third act of *La Bohème*, wrote the passage shown in Figure 61. Some singers separate the first three eighth notes of this phrase, giving each a separate syllable. They like to attack the vowel directly, which is definitely against Puccini's intention and can be avoided with a little practice.

I have now described the main features and problems of Italian phonetics and singing diction. As a postscript to this section, I here present two popular Italian arias transcribed into phonetic characters.

PHONETIC TRANSCRIPTION OF MIMI'S ARIA FROM THE FIRST ACT OF "LA BOHEME"

mi kja:manɔ mimi:, ma il mi:ɔ nnome ɛ llutʃi:a. la storja mi:a ɛ bbrɛːve. a tela‿a seta rika:mɔ in ka:za ɔ

Men - tre o pri - ma - ve - ra c'è com-pa - gno il sol:

Figure 61. Puccini, *La Bohème*

fwɔ:ri. sɔn trankwilla e‿llje:ta ed ɛ‿mmiɔ zvagɔ far
dʒiʎiʎi e‿rrɔzɛ. mi pja:tʃɔn kwelle kɔzɛ kɛ‿an si doltʃɛ
mali:a, kɛ pparlanɔ d'amo:r, di primave:rɛ, kɛ pparlanɔ
di soʎi e di kime:rɛ, kwelle kɔzɛ kɛ‿an nnome poezi:a.
lei m'intende?

mi kja:manɔ mimi:, il perke: nɔn sɔ. Sola, mi fɔ il
prantsɔ da mmɛ stɛ:ssa. Non va:dɔ sempre a me:ssa ma
prɛgɔ‿assai il siɲor. Vi:vɔ so:la, sole:tta, la in u:na
bjanka kamere:tta gwardɔ su:i te:tti e‿in tʃɛ:lɔ. ma
kwandɔ vjen lɔ zdʒe:lɔ il pri:mɔ so:le‿ɛ mmi:ɔ! il
pri:mɔ ba:tʃɔ dell' apri:le ɛ mmi:ɔ! il pri:mɔ so:le‿ɛ
mmi:ɔ! dʒermɔʎʎa‿in un va:zɔ una rɔza, ffɔʎʎa‿a
ffɔʎʎa la spi:ɔ! Kɔzi: dʒenti:l il profu:mɔ d'un fjor! Ma‿
i fjor ki:ɔ ffatʃtʃɔ ai mmɛ! non annɔ odore!
Altrɔ di mmɛ nɔn lɛ sapre:i narra:rɛ. sonɔ la su:a
vitʃi:na ke la vvjen fwɔri dɔ:ra a importuna:rɛ.

PHONETIC TRANSCRIPTION OF GERMONT'S
ARIA FROM THE SECOND ACT OF "LA TRAVIATA"

di provɛntsa il ma:r il swɔl ki dal kɔ:r ti kantʃello? ki
dal kɔ:r ti kantʃello di provɛntsa‿il provɛntsa‿il swɔ:l? Al

nati:ɔ fuldʒe:ntɛ sol kwal desti:nɔ ti furɔ? o rrammenta
pu:r nel dwɔ:l ki:vi dʒɔ:ja‿a tɛ bbrillɔ, e kɛ ppa:tʃɛ kɔla
sol su tɛ ssplendere ankor pwɔ. di:ɔ mmi gwidɔ:!
a‿il tu:ɔ vekkjɔ dʒenitɔ:r tu non sa:i kwantɔ ssɔffri:!
Tɛllonta:nɔ, di skwallo:r il suɔ tetto si kɔpri:. ma ssɛ
alfi:n ti trovɔ‿ankor, sɛ‿in mɛ sspe:mɛ non falli:, sɛ lla
vo:tʃɛ dɛll' onɔ:r in tɛ‿appje:n non ammuti:, di:ɔ
mezaudi:!

LATIN PHONETICS AND DICTION

The vocal accompanist and coach, especially those
who handle choirs, will frequently encounter sacred or
secular Latin texts. There has always been great confusion about the way to pronounce Latin, each country
pronouncing it according to its own diction: French
Latin sounds thoroughly French; German Latin is pronounced differently in Austria and in Germany; English
Latin assumes a very strange twang in the United States;
and our English and Irish cousins pronounce it with a
distinct accent of their own.

Only during the last few decades has a definite change
taken place. Latin pronunciation has been established

by the Roman Catholic Church for the whole Roman Catholic world and lay people have accepted the Church's ruling.

The first edict of a pope concerning this matter was issued in 1903. Pius X, who in his "Motu Proprio" had initiated a complete reform of church music, decided also to admonish his priests to pronounce the Latin exactly like the Italian, and, more correctly, like the Roman pronunciation of Italian. These reforms took time to seep down to the lower levels of the Church.

In 1912, Pius X wrote to Louis Du Bois, Archbishop of Bourges, saying: "We learn . . . with real pleasure that this reform has already spread to a number of places and been successfully introduced into many cathedral churches, seminaries and colleges and even into simple country churches. The question of the pronunciation of Latin is closely tied up with that of the restoration of the Gregorian Chant, the constant subject of Our thoughts, and recommendations from the very beginning of Our Pontificate. The accent and pronunciation of Latin had great influence on the melodic and rhythmic formation of the Gregorian phrase and consequently it

is important that these melodies should be rendered in the same manner in which they were artistically conceived at their first beginning. Finally the spread of the Roman pronunciation will have the further advantage . . . of consolidating more and more the work of liturgical union in France, a unity to be accomplished by the happy return to Roman liturgy and Gregorian Chant. This is why We desire that the movement of return to the Roman pronunciation of Latin should continue with the same zeal and consoling success which has marked its progress hitherto."

In 1919, the Cardinal Secretary of State, Gasparri, wrote to an abbot in Spain: "In His unending solicitude the Holy Father has not lost sight of the happy and timely initiative taken by you a few years ago by your introduction in your Monastery of the Roman pronunciation of Latin in order to bring about the desired uniformity.

"His Holiness, having resolved to insist on this point in Spain and in other countries, would be very happy to learn what reception has been given to this wise reform . . ."

And on November 30, 1928, Pope Pius XI wrote to the same Louis Du Bois, who in the meantime had become a Cardinal and the Archbishop of Paris:

". . . We also esteem very greatly your plan of urging all who come under your jurisdiction to pronounce Latin *more romano*. Not content like Our predecessors of happy memory, Pius X and Benedict XV, simply to approve his pronunciation of Latin, We, Ourselves, express the keenest desire that all bishops *of every nation* shall endeavor to adopt it when carrying out the liturgical ceremonies." (Italics mine.)

If Latin singing diction is to be exactly the same as Italian singing diction, clearly all phonetic rules for Italian remain valid for Latin. There are, however, a few additional sounds in Latin which must be dealt with briefly.

The y is pronounced as i.

The semivowel [j] is pronounced the same way as in the Italian word ieri which in earlier days was spelled jeri.

The diphthongs ae and oe are pronounced like the Italian [ɛ].

Dies *irae*, dies illa solvet saecula in favilla. Coelum et terrae ([tʃeːlum et tɛrrɛ])

The double consonant x [ks] is encountered frequently. It is pronounced like a voiced g and z in initial syllable sounds when it is preceded by an e and followed by another vowel, or when an h or s is interjected between the x and the following vowel.

Domine exaudi orationem meam ([ɛgzaudi])

In all other cases the x is pronounced like voiceless k and s.

Gloria in excelsis Deo ([ɛkstʃɛlsɪs])

The h is a frequent initial sound in Latin, but according to the pope's ruling it must be mute, exactly as it is in Italian.

Some oratorios and operatic works written in Latin use the Greek pronunciation, which is the pronunciation taught in German high schools and colleges. For instance, Stravinsky's *Oedipus Rex* and some of Orff's compositions are expressly spelled in the Greek manner. Since the musical idea was conceived in that way, the accompanist or coach should not Italianize pronunciation.

The following example of phonetic spelling of the "Dies Irae" should suffice to make the *more romano* pronunciation altogether clear to the accompanist and coach.

PHONETIC TRANSCRIPTION OF
"DIES IRAE"

diːes iːrɛ, diːes illa, sɔlvet sɛklum in faviːlla: teste daːvid kum sibiːlla. kwantus tremɔr ɛst futuːrus, kwandɔ juːdeks ɛst ventuːrus kunkta striktɛ diskusuːrus! tuːba miːrum spardʒens sɔːnum per sepulkra redʒioːnum, kɔdʒɛt ɔmnes antɛ tːoːnum.

mɔrs stupeːbit et natuːra, kum resurdʒɛt kreatuːra, judikanti responsuːra.

liːber skriptus profereːtur, in kwo tɔtum cɔntineːtur, unde murdus juditʃeːtur.

juːdeks ergɔ kum sedeːbit kwidkwid laːtet appareːbit, nil inultum remane bit.

kwid sum miːzer tunk diktuːrus? kum viks justus sit sekuːrus.

rɛks tremendɛ: majestaːtis, kwi salvandis salvas graːtis.

sɔlva me, fons pietaːtis.

rekordaːre jeːzu piːɛ, kwɔd sum kauːza tuɛ viːɛ ne me perdas illa diːɛ.

kwerens me, sedisti lassus: redɛmisti krutʃɛm passus: tantus laːbɔr non sit kassus.

juste juːdeks ultsioːnis, doːnum fak remissioːnis; ante diːem ratsioːnis.

indʒemiːskɔ, tamkwam reːus, kulpa ruːbet vultus meːus supplikanti partʃe deːus.

kwi mariːam abzɔlviːsti, et latroːnum ɛgzaudiːsti miːi kwokwe spem dediːsti.

pretʃes meːɛ non sunt dinɛ; zed tu boːnus fak beniːɲe, ne perenni kreːmer iɲe.

inter oːves loːkum preːsta, et ab edis me sɛkweːstra staːtuens in parte dekstra. kɔnfutaːtis malediːktis, flammis aːkribus addiːktis, voːka me kum benediːktis.

orɔ suppleks et akkliːnis, kɔr kɔntriːtum kwaːzi tʃiːnis, dʒeːrɛ kuːram meːi fiːnis.

lakrimoːza diːes illa, kwaː: resurdʒɛt ɛks favilla. judikandus oːmɔ reːus, uːik ergɔ partʃe deːus. piːɛ jeːzu doːmine, doːna eːis reːkwiɛm. aːmɛn.

French Phonetics and Diction

FRENCH is a much more complicated language, phonetically, than Italian. This will become evident to anybody who compares the number of phonetic vowel sounds. There are sixteen such sounds in French, fifteen in English, fourteen in German, and seven in Italian.

The English-speaking singer will find the whole group of vowels, as well as the array of velar (nasal) sounds which are so characteristic of the French, difficult to master. Other problems, to name but a few, are the h and r sounds, the semivowels, and the liaisons.

A conscientious accompanist and coach must have a thorough working knowledge of French, the product of long study under qualified observation, and must continue to practice self-observation. As in all phonetic studies, a tape recorder will be very helpful to him. With it, he can not only listen to his own diction but demon-strate faulty pronunciation to a singer and thus make him aware of the correct pronunciation.

Speaking and singing diction are even more different from each other in French than in Italian. The greater number of vowels plus the nasal sounds, the r, and many other French phonetic qualities require adjustment when sung. The intelligent French artist himself sings his language differently from the way he speaks it. As in Italian, the vast number of regional dialects forces the singer to accept a uniform pronunciation. I have chosen the French of the cultured Parisian (not the slang or argot) as the best standard for singing in French. This may be exemplified by the manner of pronouncing the r. For vocal purposes, the nasal sounds must also be adjusted. If the velum is lowered too much, as it is in speaking, the resonance switches from the mouth to the nose and an uneven, exaggerated way of singing

[48]

French words results. Moreover open and closed vowels must fit the vocal line, especially in classical music. Nothing is worse than to change vocal color from tone to tone, as spoken diction sometimes warrants.

In general, it may be said that French singing diction conforms to the rules of the Italian bel canto — with the unavoidable exceptions, of course, that result from the peculiarities of the French language. Correct pronunciation of French sounds is indispensable in order to avoid misunderstanding such words as pêcheur-pêcheur, poisson-poisson, près-prêt-pré, and many others.

VOWELS

The great number of French vowels necessitates a keen ear and a willing tongue. The differences are small. Examples must be well chosen by the accompanist and coach. Special care must be taken to explain to the singer the function of the three written accents.

French linguists differentiate several a's which — for singing purposes — they simplify to an anterior and a posterior sound. This classification is highly misleading, because every singer will associate the word posterior with backward production, which is always undesirable vocally. Every a must be pronounced forward. The difference lies in the position of lips, tongue, and jaw. The spot where a French a should be produced in singing is exactly where the Italian a is situated and the mode of production is the same (pp. 12–13). I shall distinguish, however, between long a and short a.

The long a sound. The a is long in final syllables ending in -ar, -are, -arre, -age, -ave, -asion, -assion, -ation.

Mets-le vite à ton cor*s*age. Il est fait à ton im*a*ge (DE-BUSSY "Fleurs des blés")

Mais n'apportant de p*a*ssion profonde, qu'à s'adorer (FAURE "Au Bord de l'eau")

It is long and less open in final syllables ending in -ase, -aze, -able, -acle, -asse, and in words like mac*a*bre and s*a*bre when the final r is preceded by a voiced consonant.

C'est l'ext*a*se langoureuse (DEBUSSY song)
De sa dent soudaine et vor*a*ce (DUPARC "Le Manoir de Rosemonde")

In words like pl*a*ce, m*a*sse, and ch*a*sse, the a is short. This is an exception to the above rule.

Place, place au seigneur Alcade (BIZET *Carmen*)
La nuit qui tombe et chasse la troupe (DEBUSSY "Chevaux de bois")

â (with circumflex accent) is also long and comparatively closed as in mâtin, pâle, grâce.

In endings on -âmes, -âtes, and -ât the a is short.
a is long but open in nouns and adjectives derived from or composed by the syllable -as, as in *las, lasser, pas* (step), *passer*, etc.

Tes beaux yeux sont *las*, pauvre amante (DEBUSSY "Le Jet d'eau")

In endings on -as of the second person singular the a is short as in tu viendr*as*.
a is long and rather closed in some words on -as, such as the adverb *pas* (not), *parias, bras, chas*.

Je lui disais: Tu m'aimer*as*.
Aussi longtemps que tu pourr*as*.
Je ne dormais bien qu'en ses br*as* (CHAUSSON "Chanson perpetuelle")
Fille du Par*ia* (DELIBES *Lakmé*)

The a is also long in words like casser, classe, tasse, damner, condamner (the m is mute in these last two).

Que la sort te condamne (GOUNOD *Faust*)

The a is also long in endings on -ail and -aille, as in taille, bataille, etc.

Aux vautours, il faut la bataille, pour frapper d'estoc et de taille (GOUNOD *Roméo et Juliette*)

The word méd*aille* is an exception. Its a is short.

O sainte méd*aille* (GOUNOD *Faust*)

a followed by a single n or m in the same syllable changes to the nasal [ã].
a's must be sung long but very open before a final r, z, or v, as in rare, sage, cave.

The short a sound. The short open a is found in words in which the a has an accent grave as in voilà, là, déjà, holà, etc.

Ils ont fui les longs soirs moroses déjà le jardin parfumé (CHAMINADE "Viens, mon bien-aimé")

In endings on -ac, -ak, and -aque.

Et dans les flaques d'eau retentissaient mes pas (POULENC "Air romantique")

Et ses jambes faisaient clic-clac (OFFENBACH *Les Contes d'Hoffmann*)

In endings on -at, -atte, -ap, -ape, -appe, -af, -afe, -aphe, -ache.

Votre tourterelle vous échappera (GOUNOD *Roméo et Juliette*)
On viendra l'arracher (MASSENET *Manon*)

Final a's, as in ma, ta, la, va, sera are short and open. The a in monosyllabic words such as car, bal, mal is also short.

Je suis le spectre de la rose que tu portais au bal (BERLIOZ *Le Spectre de la rose*)
Et cependant, c'est mal (MASSENET *Manon*)

The a in août is mute.

The e sounds. For singing purposes we have to differentiate between three e sounds with three subtypes (not counting diphthongs and nasal sound combinations). These are the wide-open e [ɛ], the open e [ɛ], the intermediate e [ɛ], the closed e, the weak e [ə], and the mute e [ə].

In French singing diction, the ê and è sounds are not quite the same. The ê sound should be even more open than the open è vowel. Both are expressed phonetically by the symbol [ɛ]

The wide-open e sound. The wide-open e is encountered in words spelled with ê (circumflex accent). It is pronounced somewhat like — in an exaggerated way — the English bad. Words pronounced thus are tête, mêler, bête, rêve, naître.

Je rêve aux amours défunts (DEBUSSY "Nuits d'étoiles")
Ta fenêtre vide où ne brille plus ta tête charmante et ton doux sourire (CHAUSSON "Printemps triste")

The open e sound. The open e is found in words with è (grave accent), as in près, succès, père, mère, also in maire, chaise, etc. It matches exactly the Italian [ɛ] but in a somewhat exaggerated way. Also in monosyllables mes, tes, ses, les, es, when sung; in endings on -et, -ets, -ect.

The conjunction et (and) is an exception. The e is closed. Similarly, e is closed in some words like Nazareth.

Du temps de nos pères, des blancs descendirent dans cette île (RAVEL "Chansons madécasses")
Tes yeux, tes traîtres yeux sont clos (D'INDY "Lied Maritime")

Qu'elle puisse connaître l'émoi qu'elle fait naître (GOUNOD *Faust*)

Generally, it can be said that the e in French is always open in words with syllables that end with a consonant whether this consonant is pronounced or just expressed by spelling, with the exception of syllables ending in -ez or -er (which have a closed e).

The wide open and open e's are long before final r, [z], [ʒ], and v when they are pronounced, as in colère, aise, neige, paisible, seize.

Puis, chez nous, tout heureux, tout aises (BERLIOZ "Villanelle")
Il neige, il neige (BEMBERG "Il neige")
Et vous, paisibles vallons, adieu (TCHAIKOVSKY *Jeanne d'Arc*)

e is short before all other consonants that appear in the same syllable. This is also true for the vowel combinations ai, aî, ei, and ey, pronounced like open e's.

The words aile, aime, and baisse are long.

Je t'aime et meurs, ô mes amours, Mon âme en baisers m'est ravie (FAURE "Lydia")
Mon bonheur renaît sous ton aile (BACHELET "Chère Nuit")

The intermediate e sound. The intermediate e, still expressed phonetically by [ɛ], is somewhat less open than the [ɛ] in père. Its English counterpart may be found in the words set and bell. In French, it is pronounced when an e is found before two or three consonants, as in descendre, faible, laisser, parfait, merci, peste, permettre, espoir, terminer.

Bon Saint Michel veuillez descendre (RAVEL "Chanson épique")
La peste! Décidement vous avez la main leste (BIZET *Carmen*)

The e is also intermediate in endings on -ec, -ef, -el, -elle, -em, -en, -ex, as in avec, chef, harem, etc., when the final consonant is pronounced.

Le mien devient un chef fameux (BIZET *Carmen*)
Leurs becs sont aiguisés (GOUNOD *Roméo et Juliette*)

In the word clef the f is mute and the e, therefore, changes into a closed e.

Voici la clef, je croix (GOUNOD *Faust*)

The e is also intermediate in Noël.

Voici Noël petits enfants (WEKERLIN "Voici Noël")

e followed by a single m or n in the syllable changes to the nasal sounds [ɛ̃] or [ɑ̃]. The intermediate e is always short.

e in the middle of a word followed by mm, nm, or nn sometimes changes into a short a as in femme, prudemment, indemnité, solennelle. In other such cases the e does not change, as in ennemi, where it becomes intermediate or in ennui where it changes into the nasal [ɑ̃] sound.

Mais viendra le jour des adieux car il faut que les femmes pleurent (FAURE "Les Berceaux")

Faisons, and all imperfect forms such as faisais, have the weak e [ə].

The closed (é) [e̅ *sound*. The term "closed e" should not be taken to mean that the throat must close in order to produce it. It is only relatively more closed than the [ɛ]'s. The lower jaw is extended slightly less downward. But the accompanist and coach must take pains to make sure that the singer does not "spread" the sound. The tongue should still be low and the corners of the lips should not be extended outward. This closed e sound exists in English, as in the words chaotic and chaos, but

it is difficult for an English-speaking singer, and one hears more faulty pronunciation of this than of any other vowel. This is especially true for verb endings on -er.

German-speaking singers have no difficulty at all with the closed e. It is exactly the same as in the word leben. The Italians use it in their words eh' and deh.

The closed e in French is usually expressed by é (acute accent), as in blé, désir, été.

Dans ton coeur dort un clair de lune
Un doux clair de lune d'été (DUPARC "Chanson triste")
O grands désirs, inapaisés (BERLIOZ "Absence")

The e is also closed in nouns and adjectives ending on -er and -ier where the r is mute.

J'avais tes cheveux comme un collier noir autour de ma nuque et sur ma poitrine (DEBUSSY "La Chevelure")
Oh que ton jeune amour, ce papillon léger (FAURE "Les Roses d'Ispahan")

If the r is pronounced, the e changes to an intermediate [ɛ], as in hier, mer, cher, and enfer.

Elle à la mer, nous au tombeau (DEBUSSY "Beau Soir")
Le ciel, l'enfer ce que tu veux (PIERNE "A Lucette")

In verb endings of the first conjugation on -er and -ier (parler and prier), the e is also closed.

Et mes mains sont lasses de prier (DEBUSSY "De Fleurs")
J'irai danser la Séguédille (BIZET Carmen)

If the final r must be sounded because of a liaison, the e before becomes an intermediate [ɛ].

Les deux oiseaux siffler et chanter à la fois (DEBUSSY "Voici que le Printemps")

In endings on -ez, -ied, -ieds, if the final consonants are mute as in nez, assez, croyez, pied, assieds, the e is closed.

Son pied sur le clair parquet (MASSENET "Première Danse")

If the final consonant is pronounced, the e changes into an intermediate [ɛ] as in Cortez.

The weak e [ə] *sound*. The weak e has no direct counterpart in English. It is similar to the e sound in herb, but produced more forward and without any trace of the following r. It is also similar to the short ö in German, but it is weaker and less stressed. The weak e is produced with slightly protruding and rounded lips with the tongue's sides curling upward.

The e is weak in syllables ending with e, as in je, te, ce, de, retour, venir, ceci, cela, dehors.

Va! je te hais (BIZET Carmen)
Carmen! Carmencita! Cela revient au même (BIZET Carmen)

If re- as an initial syllable followed by two or three consonants is not a prefix but belongs to the root of the word, the e has the intermediate sound, as in respirer, ressuciter.

The mute e [ə] *sound*. The mute e is only a subtype of the weak e. This also extends to the plural of verbs and adjectives on -es, as in mèr(es), ell(es), and the second person plural and the third person plural of verbs on -es and -ent, as in tu aim(es), ils aim(ent).

Accompanists and coaches must clear up confusion among their pupils about the ending on -ent of adverbs or nouns which are pronounced with nasal en (notablement, moment) and the third person plural endings of verbs which are mute – ils aim(ent), ils aimai(ent), aimèr(ent), aimerai(ent), aimass(ent).

[54]

In speech there are many very complicated rules covering when a [ə] should or should not be pronounced — i.e., when it becomes mute. In singing diction these rules become more or less simplified by the way the composers handle the [ə]. It is most frequently found in endings — mère, elle, porte, j'aime, etc. None of these final e's is pronounced in everyday speech. They must be pronounced, however, in singing if they are placed under a long note or under a note which differs from the preceding note (see Figs. 62 and 63). Otherwise, the

Figure 62. Bizet, *Carmen*, example of a mute e which must be sung

Figure 63. Massenet, *Thaïs*, example of a mute e which must be sung

e is mute. But here a distinction must be made between classical and modern music. In classical music, final e's even on short notes or on the same pitch as the preceding

note should still get a very small amount of sound. This sound had best be given to the preceding consonant, as in the carefully spoken English words, sound, lag. But even voiceless consonants should receive a little of the mute e in classical music. Weak final e's following another vowel as in poupée, bleue, vie, rue, receive the same treatment; the music will decide whether or not it should become mute (Fig. 64).

Figure 64. Debussy, "Nous n'avons pas de maison"

Things are different in modern music. Here, the final e may be entirely mute if put under the same short note (Fig. 65). Within a sentence, the e which is frequently mute in speaking can also become mute or be elided in singing, mostly in operettas, popular music, or music with a strong colloquial flavor (Figs. 66–68).

Figure 65. Poulenc, "L'Écrevisses"

elided in words like eau, asseoir, tombeau, beaucoup, where the e is only an orthographic relic. The e is also elided when it stands between a [ʒ] sound and another vowel, as in affligeant, geôlier, Georges.

Le geôlier dort (GOUNOD *Faust*)

Final weak e is also elided when a liaison is made from it to another initial vowel.

La mer est infinie et mes rêves sont fous (FAURE "La Mer est infinie")

The eu [ø], [œ] sounds. The eu sounds are long and closed [ø], and short and open [œ]. Phonetically, they are not diphthongs but vowels. They are not found in English, but they exist in German as ö. They are produced in a way similar to the [ə] sound. Since their place in the phonetic diagram is halfway between e and o, they should be practiced by vocalizing an o and then protruding and rounding the lips, gradually changing into an [ø]. The same exercise should then be continued beginning with [ə] (with lips slightly less protruded) to an intermediate e (with lips relaxed). The same process may then be reversed — e to ə to ø to o.

un p'tit bonhomm', un p'tit bonhomm', un p'tit bonhomm' pas plus haut qu'ça

Figure 66. Offenbach, *Madame L'Archiduc*

Un p'tit noir?   Moi,   j'ai eu ch'vaux et voi-

Figure 67. Charpentier, *Louise*

Dir' qu'en c'mo-ment   y a des   femmes qui   dorment

Figure 68. Charpentier, *Louise*

Under all circumstances the [ə] must be pronounced in monosyllables which are followed by an aspirated h and cannot, therefore, be connected by liaison, as in le héro. The [ə] is also pronounced lightly before the word rien, as in je ne demande rien. When the [ə] stands between two consonants on one side and one consonant on the other side, it must always be pronounced for euphonic reasons, as in "Voici notre repas," from Massenet's *Manon*.

The mute e may be called elided if not even a trace of it is retained in pronouncing a word. The e is always

The open eu [œ] is produced the same way except for a much larger rounded opening of the mouth and slight dropping of jaw and tongue (Fig. 19).

The closed eu [ø] sound. All [ø] sounds are to be pronounced long. This sound, which may also be spelled oeu, can be found in three places.

First, at the end of words (dieu, feu, jeu, peu, queue, bleue), or with a final mute consonant or consonants as in words ending in -eux, oeufs, boeufs, neufs (new), pleut, peut, monsieur, messieurs.

Secondly, it is found in endings followed by consonants that are pronounced, as in jeûne, and in endings on -euse, -eute, and -eutre.

Ouvre tes yeux bleus ma mignonne (MASSENET "Ouvre tes yeux bleus")

Elle est dangereuse (BIZET *Carmen*)

Déjeune, derived from jeûne, is pronounced more open.

Thirdly, eu in the middle of a word is closed and long in words such as deuxième, lieutenant, bleuir, jeudi, meunier, and in adverbs ending in -eusement.

Mon officier n'est pas capitaine; pas même lieutenant (BIZET *Carmen*)

De blé le grenier est plein, le meunier fait sentinelle (PIERNE "Le Moulin")

The open eu [œ] sound. This sound is actually an intensified [ə] sound. It may also be spelled oeu. It is found and pronounced short in words where it is followed by the consonants f, g, l, n, p as in neuf (nine), oeuf (see exception in plural forms above), aveugle, seul, peuple, jeune.

Je suis seul! Seul enfin (MASSENET *Manon*)
Mais quelquefois le souvenir du jugement injuste et aveugle des hommes (MILHAUD "A la lune")

If followed by the consonants r and v, eu is still open but long, as in coeur, beurre, leur, sieur, pleure, soeur, oeuvre, fleuve, oeil, deuil.

Dans ton coeur dort un clair de lune (DUPARC "Chanson triste")

Il pleure dans mon coeur comme il pleut sur la ville (DEBUSSY "Il pleure dans mon coeur")

In heureux [œrø:], the first syllable is slightly less open than in heure.

Forms of the verb avoir spelled with eu elide the e, such as in j'eus (pronounced [ʒy]), eu ([y]), j'eusse, etc.

J'eus un moment de tristesse (MASSENET *Manon*)

The i and y sound. The French i, in some cases spelled y, is a closed vowel. That does not mean — I must stress this again and again — that its production by a singer requires closing the throat. There just is no other term that would describe as well the function of some sounds.

The i is produced the same way as the Italian i, and the dangers of spreading and of a pushed, metallic sound are the same (pp. 14–15 show description and production). One could also say that the French i and y are exactly the same as the vowel sounds in the English words sea and key.

There are two kinds of i in French, the long and the short. Final i's are moderately short, as in ami, si, lit, lys, riz, radis, ici, hardi.

Nous avons des *lits* pleins d'odeurs légères (DEBUSSY "La Mort des amants")
La fauvette dans les vallons a laissé son am*i* fidèle (BIZET "Vieille Chanson")
Sur un lys pâle mon coeur dort (DUPARC "Extase")

The i is somewhat longer in p*is*, puis, minuit.

i is short before consonants except r, [z], [ʒ], [ɲ], and [v], as in pipe, huit, riche, captif, profiter, fils.

Ah, mon f*i*ls (MEYERBEER *Le Prophète*)
Prof*i*tons bien de la jeunesse (MASSENET *Manon*)
BUT: Songe à la douceur d'aller là bas v*i*vre ensemble (DUPARC "L'Invitation au voyage")

î follows the same rules, as in île, huître.
i is long before r, [z], [ʒ], [ɲ], and [v], as in mourir, rire, lyre, brise, vertige, digne, and rive.

Je ne suis pas d*i*gne de vous (MASSENET *Manon*)
La voile enfle son aile, la brise va souffler (BERLIOZ "Les Nuits d'été")
Triste lyre soupire (DEBUSSY "Nuits d'étoiles")

In endings on ie the i is lengthened somewhat by the weak or mute e.

Allons, enfants de la patr*ie* ("La Marseillaise")

ï in words like haïr means simply a division into two syllables and therefore it remains i.

i followed by a single n or m in the same syllable changes into the nasal [ɛ̃].

The o sounds. o in French may be closed or open, long or short. It may also be spelled au or eau; in these cases it is always long. The French vowel sound o does not exist in English, which diphthongizes the o, but it does exist in Italian and German. (See pp. 15 and 16 for detailed description of production of the two o's.) In French speech the o's are pronounced in a rather guttural way. This must not be done in singing. Forward production is as essential here as anywhere else.

The closed o [o] *sound.* Final [o] is closed and long as in oh, mot, tôt, nôtre, eau, faux, chaud, trop, bravo, repos, un os, des os.

Un chaud parfum circule, repose ô Phidylé (DUPARC "Phidylé")

Les *eaux* sur les grands *saules* coulent (DUPARC "Au Pays où se fait la guerre")

The word dot has an open o ([ɔ]); the final t is pronounced. In some idiomatic phrases such as pot-au-feu, mot-à-mot, the first o is open.

In the middle of a word the o is closed and long or moderately long in words where it has a circumflex accent (trône), before a [z] (rose, generosité) and when it is followed by the suffix -tion as in emotion, devotion. If expressed by au, the o is likewise closed and long when followed by a consonant other than r, as in cruauté, beaucoup.

Sourbillonnent dans l'extase d'une lune *rose* et *grise* (DEBUSSY "Mandoline")

The closed short o, which exists in Italian as in bocca, is not known in French.

o is closed and long in grossir, dossier, rôtir, odeur, obus, arome, exauce.

Exauce ma prière (GOUNOD *Faust*)

The open o [ɔ] *sound.* Initial o is open and short when it has no circumflex accent and is not followed by an s plus vowel, as in orange, hostil.

In the middle of a word it is open and short before all consonants, as in bloc, noce, étoffe, coq, propre, poste, cloche, notre, loge, robe, homme, donne, école, ivrogne, Rome.

Les *cloches* tintaient légères et franches (DEBUSSY "Les Cloches")

Et que les *hommes* curieux tentent les horizons (FAURE "Les Berceaux")

Un *ivrogne* qui dort (OFFENBACH *Les Contes d'Hoffmann*)

o is open but long in all endings on -or and -orre with or without a final mute consonant, as in abord, encore, tort, abhorre, effort, fort.

Le bois embaumé semble dormir encore (MASSENET "Les Oiselets")
Un fort menaçant s'éleva (RAVEL "Chansons madé-casses")

o followed by a single n or m in the same syllable changes to the nasal sound [õ]. o followed by a syllable starting with another vowel is frequently closed slightly for reasons of assimilation, as in poème and coalition.

au before an r is always more open than the au would be otherwise, and long, as in aurore, taureau, j'aurai, restaure, mauvais.

Aussi me trouves — tu toujours à chaque aurore tout en pleurs (FAURÉ "Le Papillon et la fleur")
Nous venions de voir le taureau (DELIBES "Les Filles de Cadix")

The name Paul (but not Pauline) has an open au.
The ou [u] sound. Ou in French speech is pronounced rather backward. In singing diction, we again revert to the pure bel canto way of production as in Italian. (See p. 17.) It is pronounced as in the English doom, but without the slightest trace of diphthongization. In order to overcome the danger of his singers' sounding hooty or muffled the accompanist or coach should practice with them a closed [o] and progress to the [u] sound without too much change of mouth and tongue position. The u in Italian is always long. It may be long or short in French.

Final ou is long in où (where), cou, etc., and before mute final consonants such as b, bs, d, g, p, t, and x, as in radoub, joug, loup, tout, doux, and also in foule and douce.

Tout doux, monsieur, tout doux (BIZET Carmen)
L'âme du loup pleure dans cette voix (DEBUSSY "Le Son du cor s'afflige")

ou is long in stressed syllables before an r, [z], [ʒ], or [v], as in jour, amour, douze, épouse, rouge, trouve.

Le jour venait, l'astre des nuits pâlit (OFFENBACH "Le Matin")
Belle nuit, o nuit d'amour (OFFENBACH Les Contes d'Hoffmann)

Épouse au front lumineux (CHANSON "Cantique a l'épouse")

ou is short before any pronounced or mute consonant — with the exception of b, bs, d, g, l, r, t, x, v, z, [ʒ] — as in nous, vous, tousse, mousse.

Les roses d'Ispahan dans leur gaîne de mousse (FAURE "Les Roses d'Ispahan")
Vous viendrez avec nous (BIZET Carmen)

The word tous is pronounced in different ways. When it is an adjective the s is mute and the ou long, as in tous les jours, tous les hommes. Where tous is used as a pronoun it is pronounced [tus]. The s is sounded and the ou short.

Ici-bas tou(s) les hommes (FAURE "Ici-bas")
Je vous invite tous (BIZET Carmen)
Et tous s'en vont dans l'ombre et dans la lune (CHAUSSON "Les Heures")

Sometimes a circumflex accent appears on the u of the ou sound, as in coûter, goûter, etc. This does not change the pronunciation of the ou.

The u [y] sound. The u sound does not exist in English or in Italian, though it appears in German. Pronouncing it creates considerable difficulty for the English-speaking singer. The [y] is produced by pursing the lips, rounded for pronouncing an ou (see p. 17 for production of the [u]). The position of mouth and lips is not unlike the preparation for whistling. The tongue is higher than in pronouncing the ou. The accompanist or coach will have to explain the [y] to the singer by describing the position of the lips and by emphasizing the fact that the [y] lies halfway between [u] and [i]. The singer should practice holding one tone while changing from [u] to [y] to [i], at the same time fixing in his mind the exact position for the different sounds.

The [y] is long before r, [z], [ʒ], and [v], as in pur, ruse, déluge, étuve.

L'amour est pur comme la flamme (BEMBERG "Elaine")
Cinq ans! et pas de leçon mais c'est rusé dame (MASSENET "Première Danse")

[y] is short or at best moderately long in most other cases, as in tu, nue, lutte, fut, rue, Jésus, plus, salut, lune.

La lune blanche luit dans les bois (HAHN "L'Heure exquise")

Salut, demeure chaste et pure (GOUNOD *Faust*)
Aussitôt qu'on aime où est Jésus même (CHARPENTIER "Prière")

The circumflex accent does not change the length of the [y], as in fûmes, fût, flûte.

Et tour à tour nos bouches s'unissent sur la fl*û*te
(DEBUSSY "La Flûte de Pan")

Syllables in which the u is followed by n or m are nasalized [œ̃].

In the exclamation chut, the u is almost completely suppressed.

Ch*u*t! Le voilà (GOUNOD *Faust*)

NASAL VOWEL SOUNDS

There are four nasal vowel sounds: [ɑ̃], [õ], [œ̃], and [ɛ̃]. These sounds do not exist in English, Italian, or German. They are produced by lowering the velum (soft palate) a little so that the stream of air will partly escape through the nasal passages and partly through the mouth. This lowering of the velum must not be exaggerated because the result would be an ugly nasal sound which would mar language and tone. The position of

mouth, lips, and jaw remains unchanged for the nasal vowels. A singer should use as little nasality as is possible. The positions correspond to those for the original vowels, [a], [o], [œ], and [ɛ], which must never lose their identity. Here the n and m are blended into the nasal vowel and are not pronounced by themselves. Sang is pronounced [sɑ̃] in French and not [saŋ]. The accompanist or coach must make it clear to the singers that these nasal vowels are not like the English nasal consonants, as in long, sing, where nasality is effected on the n and g sounds. The consonants following a nasal sound must be pronounced as late as possible, as in songer ([sõ:ʒe]).

Figure 69 shows place of the four nasal vowels in simple diagram form. The nasal vowels are either long or moderately long, never really short. Initial nasal vowels should be attacked softly, without any glottal stroke.

The [ɑ̃] *sound.* This sound is produced initially the same way as the vowel a. The mouth must be wide open. Then the velum is lowered slightly.

The [ɑ̃] is long when followed by a consonant other

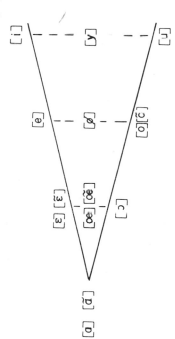

Figure 69. Diagram showing the four French nasal vowels

than n or m in the next syllable, as in blanche, grande, langue.

La lune blanche Luit dans les bois (HAHN "L'Heure exquise")

Adieu, notre petite table, si grande pour nous cependant (MASSENET *Manon*)

Damner and bannir are not nasalized.

Il voudrait en vain de son âme pouvoir me chasser, me bannir (SAINT-SAENS *Samson et Dalila*)

[ɑ̃] is medium long in all other cases, as in banc, temps, dedans, champs.

Voici venir les temps où vibrant sur sa tige (DEBUSSY "Harmonie du soir")

Et qu'un tiède frisson court sur les champs de blé (DEBUSSY "Beau Soir")

The words faon and paon elide the o and nasalize the an ([fɑ̃], [pɑ̃]), as, for example, in the title of Ravel's song, "Le Paon."

Initial en is pronounced [ɑ̃] before a consonant other than n or m, as in ensemble and entends.

Ensemble, relisons (MASSENET *Manon*)

Je l'entends rire et je vois luire (BIZET "Sérénade")

In ennui, ennoblir, emmener, etc., notwithstanding the double n or m, the pronunciation is [ɑ̃]. Not so, however, in ennemi, or hennir (also pronounced hannir).

Interior en or em is pronounced [ɑ̃] when followed by a consonant other than n or m, as in ensemble, temple, cadence, entente, also in endings on -ention, -entiel.

Final en is pronounced [ɑ̃] when followed by a mute consonant as in temps, souvent, entends.

Nous avons dit souvent d'impérissables choses (DEBUSSY "Le Balcon")

Il en est *temps* encore (GOUNOD *Faust*)

Some words of foreign derivation are nasalized; for such, consult a phonetic dictionary.

The [ɛ̃] *sound*. The [ɛ̃] is produced the same way as the open [ɛ] but with the velum slightly lowered so that nasality is produced.

Initial in sounds are nasalized before a single consonant as in i*n*fame, i*n*fortune, i*n*connu, i*m*prégner. These [ɛ̃]'s are long.

Et de bonheur à l'i*n*fortune (MILHAUD "L'Innocence")
Quelque i*n*connu (MASSENET *Manon*)

Initial in and im, when followed by a vowel or by another n or m, are not nasalized, as in image, inutile, immense, innovation.

Dans un sommeil que charmait ton *image* (FAURE "Après un rêve")
Devant l'*im*mensité ton extase s'éveille (FAURE "Rencontre")

The word hymne is also not nasalized.
Exceptions to the above rule are immangeable, immanquable, which nasalize the initial im.

Interior in sounds are nasalized before a consonant other than n or m, as in crainte, vainqueur, Olympia, nymphe, timbre. They are always pronounced moderately long.

L'Amour *vain*queur et la vie opportune (FAURE "Clair de lune")
Je vous présente ma fille Oly*m*pia (OFFENBACH *Les Contes d'Hoffmann*)

Final in sounds in any of the above-listed spellings are nasalized with or without a terminating consonant, as in faim, thym, rein, saint, cinq, main, lynx, point, poing. They are of medium length.

Ne les déchirez pas avec vos deux *mains* blanches (DEBUSSY "Green")
Et le *poing* sur la hanche (DELIBES "Les Filles de Cadix")

In endings on -ien or -ient, the en sound is pronounced [ɛ̃], as in mien, tien, chien, bien, païen, récipient, moyen, chrétien, viens, tiens.

Comme un chi*en* l'amour m'a mordu (DUPARC "Le Manoir de Rosemonde")
Viens mon bien-aimé (CHAMINADE "Viens mon bien-aimé")

Words ending in -ienne are not nasalized, as in Vienne, ancienne, ils viennent, etc.

The [õ] *sounds.* The [õ] sound is produced like the regular closed o (see p. 16), with nasalization by a slight lowering of the velum. It is important that the lips should be rounded and protruded, otherwise it may sound too much like [ã].

Initial on or om sounds are long, and are nasalized before a single consonant as in ombre, onde.

Comme s'en va cette *onde* (DEBUSSY "Beau Soir")
C'est l'*ombre* que j'embrasse (SAINT-SAENS "La Solitaire")

Interior on sounds are likewise nasalized before a consonant other than n or m as in monde, songe, tombeau, comte, compter, rompu, longue, blonde, honte. In these cases the on sounds are long.

In monosyllables or final syllables the on is also nasalized and is of moderate length, as in mon, fond, long, réponds, talon, applombe, romps, compt.

Le *long* du quai les grands vaisseaux (FAURE "Les Berceaux")
Ah, *réponds* à ma tendresse (SAINT-SAENS *Samson et Dalila*)

The word monsieur is pronounced [məsjø]; the n is mute. For pronunciation of paon, faon, see page 63. For pronunciation of messieurs, see page 57.

On and om before another n or m are not nasalized, as in donner, bonne, nommer, en somme, omnipotent, calomnie. In the last two cases the m is mute. (See p. 73.)

En *somme*, un vrai gentil*homme* (GOUNOD *Faust*)
Donne (GOUNOD *Faust*)
Infâme *calomnie* (MASSENET *Manon*)

The [œ̃] *sounds.* The production of the [œ̃] sound corresponds to the [œ] (see p. 57), with slightly lowered velum. It is important that the sound be kept open. The [œ̃], like the [œ], creates difficulties for the English-speaking singer. These sounds must be practiced thoroughly, if possible with the help of a tape recorder.

Initial un is only moderately long. It is nasalized in the article un, but not in une.

C'était *un* ange, *un* ange (GOUNOD *Faust*)

Interior um and un are nasalized and long before a consonant, as in humble, lundi, défunte, etc.

Et qu'à vos yeux si beau l'*humble* présent soit doux (DEBUSSY "Green")

Comme au temps des défunts amours (CHAUSSON "Nos Souvenirs")

Final un is always nasalized and moderately long, as in chacun, brun, jeun.

Chacun se paie un sou de dimanche (DEBUSSY "Chevaux de bois")
C'est un beau brun (CHARPENTIER Louise)

There is only one nasalized word ending in -um: parfum.

Le parfum en est fort (BIZET Carmen)

Other words ending in -um, such as rhum, album, are not nasalized.

The word punch, for no obvious reason, is pronounced ponch (põʃ).

Allumons le punch! (OFFENBACH Les Contes d'Hoffmann)

SEMIVOWELS

Semivowels are vowel combinations. The French language has three, expressed phonetically by [w], [j], and [ɥ]. Although they might in speech be called semiconsonants, in singing they are nearer to vowels. The overall rule for semivowels is the following: when in ordinary spelling i, y, o, and ou are preceded by a single consonant and followed by a vowel, they turn into semivowels. However, the combinations oi, ieu, and ui become semivowels even in initial form or if preceded by more than one consonant. All semivowel sounds are extremely short. As in Italian music, the French composers show by their way of writing when a vowel combination should be sung as a semivowel and when it should be separated into ordinary vowels. If words containing them are put under a single note they definitely must be sung as semivowels. If two or more notes are given to them they lose their semivocalic character. The following individual rules must therefore be checked against the words in a given song, opera, or choral work.

The [w] *semivowel.* This sound exists in English in words like suave, language, and persuasion, and is pronounced in the same manner. In French, the [w] is pronounced in vowel combinations of o and i, as in oiseau, soit, trois, droite, bois, croix.

Aimable oiseau lui disait-il (BIZET "Vieille Chanson")
Bois frissonants, ciel étoile (CHAUSSON "Chanson perpétuelle")

bois [bwa]) = [bwɑ]   oui [wi]) = [wi]

Figure 70. Pronunciation of the semivowel w

Je bois à la Stella (OFFENBACH Les Contes d'Hoffmann)

The [w] must be pronounced very quickly, giving almost the entire full value of the musical note to the following vowel. There must not be any separation (Fig. 70). This gliding from the semivowel to the vowel creates a difficulty for the English-speaking singer and should be thoroughly explained to him; he should also practice all the semivowels on notes of different lengths.

A circumflex accent on the second part of a semivowel lengthens it, as in cloître, croître.

On sent croître tor amour dans la nuit
Du vieux cloître ou s'en va se becquetant (FAURE "Dans les ruines d'une abbaye")

Words ending in oie, oye, have the [w] followed by a weak e, as in joie, proie, oye.

The English vowel y must never be interspersed between semivowel and mute e. Joie is pronounced [ʒwǝ] and not [ʒwjǝ].

[w] is also pronounced in combinations of o with in, int, and ins, as in loin, point, moins, poing. In all these cases the in sounds are nasalized. The pronunciation of moins, for instance, is [mwɛ̃].

Je bois à la joie (RAVEL "Chanson à boire")
Comme une fleur loin du soleil (BIZET "Absence")

[w] is also pronounced in vowel combinations of ou with a, e, and i, according to the above general rule, as in louange, oui, louis, etc.

Oui je suis dans son boudoir (THOMAS Mignon)
Roi du ciel et ces anges je dirai tes louanges (MEYERBEER Le Prophète)

The singing of the ou as [w] in these cases depends largely on the music. If the composer gave two or more notes to the ou plus vowel combination it retains its original vowel quality (Fig. 71, 72).

Ou followed by a, e, or i and preceded by two consonants always retains the original vowel form, as in éblou-ir, trou-ait, prou-esse.

The words moelle and poêle and their forms are pronounced [mwal], [pwal].

The [j] semivowel. This [j] sound has its parallel in

In words with ie, iè, ieu, as in pied, nièce, riens, dieu, etc., the [j] is pronounced.

Ses *pieds* se font légers et ta voix endormante (HUE "Nuits d'été")
Et bénissez le nom du *Dieu* saint de nos pères (SAINT-SAENS *Samson et Dalila*)

In words with i and weak e the pure vowels must be pronounced. Great care should be taken not to interject a [j].

Je suis encore tout étourdie [eturdi:ə] (MASSENET *Manon*)
La mer immense et la prairie, choeur immortel: Divine éternelle harmonie (BIZET "Le Matin")

In words with io, iou, iu — passion, opium — the [j] is pronounced.

Mais n'apportant de passion profonde qu'à s'adorer (FAURE "Au Bord de l'eau")

If, according to the above general rules, two consonants precede the i vowel combinations, they retain their pure vowel form, as in tri-omphe, pri-ère, cri-ant, etc. However, the [j] is used to connect the two syllables. The right pronunciation is [trijɔfə], [prijɛrə], [krijɑ̃].

Figure 71. Charpentier, *Louise,* pronunciation of the semivowel [w]

Lou-i - - sel

Figure 72. Massenet, *Manon,* pronunciation of the semivowel [w]

Qu'a-vec le jou-eur ê-prou-vé

the English y, as in you. In French it is called the yod and is very common. But in poetry and musical lyrics the composer will decide whether one or more notes should be given to the syllable containing the [j]. If one note is given a semivowel must be sung; if two notes, the syllable is divided into two parts and retains the original vowel. The above-mentioned general rules apply.

The [j] is pronounced in words with ia, iai, ian, as in diamant, diable, biais, étudiant.

Scintille, *diamant* (OFFENBACH *Les Contes d'Hoffmann*)
Cette vieille impitoyable, de force ou de gré, je crois, allait épouser le *diable* (GOUNOD *Faust*)

O toi, Dieu de lumière, comme aux jours d'autrefois exauce ma prière et combats pour tes lois (SAINT-SAENS *Samson et Dalila*)

The forms of the verb rire and lier, although they begin with only one vowel, follow the same rule, as in rions, liez, riant – pronounced [rijõ], [lije], [rijã].

Et nous étions liés pour toujours ainsi (DEBUSSY "La Chevelure")
Ah! Ah! Rions de sa fureur (SAINT-SAENS *Samson et Dalila*)

If a y stands between two vowels, it is divided orthographically into two parts, the first becomes [wa], [ɛ], or [ɥ] and is attached to the preceding vowel; the second becomes [j] and is drawn to the following vowel, as in rayon, aiyant, voyez, essayer, payer, royal, fuyant. These words are pronounced [rɛjõ], [ɛjã], [vwaje], [ɛsɛje], [pɛje], [rwajal], [fɥijã].

Il faut payer (BIZET *Carmen*)
Qu'un rayon de soleil ne doit jamais tarir (MASSENET *Le Cid*)

ay, orthographically, is also divided into two parts at the end of words like pays, abbeye, paysan, and paysage, pronounced [pɛi:], [abɛi:ə], [pɛizã:l], [pɛiza:ʒə]. The semivowel [j] should *not* be added.

Connais-tu le pays (THOMAS *Mignon*)

y by itself or as an initial sound before a vowel is pronounced like [j], as in il y a [ilja]. As an initial sound it appears mostly in words of foreign derivation, hardly ever used in the vocal literature.

At this point it is necessary to discuss the so-called l mouillé, the liquid l, which turns into the semivowel [j]. This sound is used in combinations -ail, -aille, -eil, -eille, -euil, -euille, -ouil, and -ouille, as in travail, bataille, soleil, vieille, deuil, feuille, accueillir, fenouil, bouillon.

Comme un ange blond sous le clair sol*eil* (RAVEL "Chanson des cueilleuses de lentesque")
Le d*euil* est sans raison (DEBUSSY "Il pleure dans mon coeur")
Aux vautours il faut la bat*aille* (GOUNOD *Roméo et Juliette*)

Words like cercueil, orgueilleux, cueillir are pronounced [sɛrkœj:l], [ɔrgœjø:l], [kœji:r]. These words are met with very often in vocal literature.

Et nous n'irons plus courir, et *cueill*ir les lilas en fleur (CHAUSSON "Le Temps des lilas")
Dans le cer*cueil* de blanc capitonné (CHAMINADE "L'Anneau d'argent")

In the word ai*le* the l is not liquidized.
Most words ending in -i*lle* also are pronounced with the [j] as in fami*lle*, bri*ll*er, fi*lle*, orei*lle*s, séguédi*lle*.

Occupez mon orei*lle* par vos accents prolongés. Le vent du soir se lève, la lune commence à bri*ll*er au travers des arbres de la montagne (RAVEL "Chansons madécasses")
C'est une brave fi*lle*, qui fait l'honneur à la fami*lle* (MASSENET *Manon*)

The ll is not liquid, and therefore not pronounced [j] in vi*ll*e, mi*ll*e, tranqui*ll*e, i*ll*ustre, and their derivatives.
La chère musique de la grande Vi*ll*e (CHARPENTIER *Louise*)
Soit, monsieur, mi*ll*e pistoles (MASSENET *Manon*)

The proper noun Séville should actually be liquidized, for instance when it rhymes with séguédille. But when it is rhymed with ville one gives it the ordinary ll sound.
Près des remparts de Séville ([Sevijə]), chez mon ami

Lillas Pastia, j'irai danser la Séguédi*ll*e et boire du Manzani*ll*a (BIZET *Carmen*)
BUT: Tu vas, m'a-t-elle dit, t'en aller à la vi*ll*e [vilə].
La route n'est pas longue, une fois à Séville [sevila].

Some proper names such as Villon and Milhaud may be pronounced with [j], but the ordinary pronunciation is just as correct.

The liquid l sound [j] is not related to the Italian [ʎ] sound, spelled gl.

The [ɥ] *semivowel.* This sound has no equivalent in any other language. The difficulty it creates for English-speaking singers can only be overcome by concentrated practice. It is a combination of the u ([y]) and i with the a, [e], [ɛ], [ɛ̃], [œ] or [õ] sounds but the [y] part is of extremely short duration and glides immediately into the i.

In producing the [ɥ], the lips must be rounded and protruded very far, as for the French u (see p. 61), then suddenly withdrawn and changed into a slightly spread position. This is the only occasion where I recommend even slight spreading; otherwise the semivowel will sound indistinct. The [ɥ] semivowel is not related

[70]

to the Italian ui, as in lui, which consists of two pure vowels of which the first is longer. In French, the u is very rapid and the i gets the full value of the note, similar to the oi ([w]) (Fig. 73).

puis ([py)]) = (py-i:)

Figure 73. The semivowel [ɥ]

Most [ɥ]'s appear in the ui combinations, with preceding single consonants, as in nuit, lui, suis, détruire, puisque, puissant, ernui.

Je *suis*, je *suis* le cri de joie (LALO "La Chanson de l'alouette")
Chère *nuit* aux clartés sereines (BACHELET "Chère Nuit")

[ɥ] is also pronounced in combinations of [y] with a, [e], [ε], [œ], and [õ], preceded by a single consonant, as in nuage, suaire, insinuant, juin, respectueux, concluons.

Ô *Juin*, étincelle enivrée (FAURE "Nell")

En *suivant* le *nuage* clair que la pipe jette dans l'air (OFFENBACH *Les Contes d'Hoffmann*)

If a weak e follows a [ɥ], as in pluie, the music determines whether it is pronounced or mute. When it is pronounced, however, no additional semivowel [j] must be added.

Ô bruit doux de la *pluie* (DEBUSSY "Il pleure dans mon coeur")

Some words with syllables starting with two consonants do not take the [ɥ] sound, but retain the pure vowel sounds, as in cruelle, truelle, bruire (but [brɥ:] for bruit), bruyant.

Cruelle destinée! (GOUNOD *Faust*)

In concluding the section about semivowels I want to emphasize once more that it is up to the poet and composer to decide when semivowels are to be sung. May Laird-Brown, in *Singers' French*, gives a few examples from French music for avoidance of semivowels which could be extended ad libitum:

nu-a-ge (OFFENBACH *Les Contes d'Hoffmann*)
su-a-vi-té (DEBUSSY "Romance")

dé-fi-ance (HALÉVY *La Juive*)
mari-age (BIZET *Carmen*)
radi-eux (GOUNOD *Faust*)
mélodi-euse (MASSENET *Hérodiade*)
ru-ine (OFFENBACH *Les Contes d'Hoffmann*)

CONSONANTS

The intensity with which French consonants are to be pronounced in singing lies somewhere between the German explosiveness and the American-English underplay. It conforms in general to the crispness and gentleness of the Italian consonants. There is, however, one big difference: double consonants in French receive no additional stress; they are pronounced and sung like single consonants. For this reason I shall not discuss them separately. French consonants are sometimes pronounced, sometimes mute. The numerous rules and exceptions to the rules will form the bulk of this chapter. For the definition and production of French consonants I shall refer to the Italian wherever they coincide and write about them separately wherever they differ.

The h sound. One of the cardinal differences between the Italian and the French consonants is the treatment of the h, which is always mute in Italian, whereas in French it may be either mute or aspirated. The first kind are only spelling conventions, the second kind are consonants of the glottal fricative class. The great majority of French h's are mute; the aspirated h interests us here. The initial mute h lends itself to a liaison (see p. 90). The initial aspirated h must never be tied to the preceding word but must be separated by a hiatus (see p. 90). h in combination with gh, kh, lh, nh, rh, and th may be interior or final; it is of course also mute and does not change the pronunciation of the preceding consonant. The pronunciation of the ch will be discussed in connection with the c (see p. 79).

One hard and fast rule determines when initial h is mute and when it is aspirated, but this rule requires so much philological background that it may well remain a theory for accompanists and coaches: the initial h is always mute in words of Greek or Latin origin. Most aspirated h's come from Teutonic words, though they are sometimes hardly recognizable as such.

The aspirated h *sound.* The aspirated h is found almost exclusively as an initial consonant. The only ex-

[72]

ception is the final h of exclamations like oh! and ah! which will get slight aspiration or breathiness when expressing real emotion.

Je suis perdue! Oh! Oh! (DEBUSSY *Pelléas et Mélisande*)

Initial aspirated h is strongly aspirated in words of violent emotion, such as ha! haine, haineux, je te hais. The pronunciation corresponds to the violence of an English exclamation like Oh, hell!

Je te hais! (BIZET *Carmen*)

In all other instances, the h is aspirated more or less gently—less gently in words that still have emotional impact (honte, honteux), more gently in all others. A gently aspirated h corresponds to the h in the English words home, humble. The aspirated h's are numerous. I list those most frequently found in French vocal literature (for words not contained in this list, a dictionary may be consulted): Ha!, hache, haie, haine, haineux, haïr, haler, halte!, hameau, hanche, hardi, harceler, harasser, harpe, hasard, hâte, hâter, haut (and derivatives), Hé!, hennir, héros (but *not* héroïsme, héroïne, héroïque), hideusement, Holà!, honte, honteux, honni, horde, hors, houille, houle, hourra!, Hue, huche, huit, huguenot, hurler.

Déesse charmante *h*âtes toi (MILHAUD "L'Aurore") Paraît liste fringant et les poings sur les *h*anches (DEBUSSY "Voici que le printemps")

The h in hélas is thought to be mute. There are, however, some teachers of phonetics who will break their lances for an aspirated hélas! Huit is also aspirated in its derivatives, such as huitième, but not when it is the second word in combinations like dix-huit, vingt-huit.

The m *and* mm *sounds.* For definition and production see page 22. The vowel preceding an m must never be nasalized except in the cases where am, em, om, and um stand for [ã], [ɛ̃], [õ], [œ̃] (see pp. 62–63). The final m is always nasalized with the exception of a few words of foreign origin like harem, intérim, album, Jérusalem, etc. A vowel preceding an m which is followed by b or p is combined with the m into a nasal sound, as in jambe, simple, nymphe, compte (also, as an exception, comte).

Les satyres et les ny*m*phes aussi (DEBUSSY "Le Tombeau des naïades")

Cependant l'excellent docteur Bolonais cueille avec lenteur des simples (DEBUSSY "Fantôches")

The prefix em is nasalized [ã] if followed by another m, as in emmener.

In the mn combination, the m is assimilated to the n, as in the words damner, automne. Damner, for instance, is pronounced [dane:].

Que le sort te condamne (GOUNOD *Faust*)
Mais le vent d'automne qui brame (CHAUSSON "La Dernière Feuille")

Modern diction pronounces both m and n in the following words: indemnité, calomnie, hymne, omnibus, Agamemnon, Clythemnestre.

The n *and* nn *sounds.* For definition and production see page 23. The syllables an, en, in, ain, ein, oin, on, un are nasalized (see pp. 62–64). A few endings on -en in words of Latin origin are not nasalized, as in éden, hymen. Final syllables with the above sounds followed by c, g, d, t, and s are also nasalized, as in banc, poing, quand, point, gens.

Quand ton regard tomba sur moi (CHAUSSON "Le Chasme")

Et ce jeu nouveau pourtant point ne l'embarasse (MASSENET "Première Danse")

mn, always pronounced like a single n is not nasalized with the exception of ennoblir, ennui.

L'année en vain chasse l'année (DEBUSSY *L'Enfant prodigue*)
NASALIZED: Dans l'immortel ennui du calme sidéral (FAURE "L'Horizon chimérique")

The gn *sound.* For definition and production, see page 24. Some words containing this consonant, which is called n mouillé in French, are agneau, compagnie, magnifique, montagne, digne.

Je ne suis pas digne de vous (MASSENET *Manon*)
Que de vallons et de montagnes (BERLIOZ "Absence")

For exceptions, see page 85.

The l *and* ll *sounds.* For definition and production, see page 24. There are two kinds of l in French, the normal l and the liquid l (or l mouillé). Rarely, the l is mute. The normal l is to be found as an initial, interior, or final sound.

l is normal in endings in -al, -el, -eul, -ol, -oil, as in

bal, ciel, seul, col, voile, and in the middle of words in connection with the same vowel combinations.

Si vous me disiez que l'ennui vous vient du ciel trop fleuri (RAVEL "Chanson romanesque")

Passe, passe dans un rayon tremblant en voile blanc (BERLIOZ "Au Cimitière")

l is normal in combinations of -oul and -ul as in foule, brûler, with the exception of pou(ls), sou(l) and cu(l) where the l is mute.

l in combination with -il is mostly normal, as in mil, fil, subtil, île, péril. It is mute in some words, such as genti(l), fusi(l), nombri(l), but liquid in some similar ones, such as gentilhomme, gentille.

Du mal en masse et du bien en foule (DEBUSSY "Chevaux de bois")

D'un sillage d'argent des îles de la sonde (FAURE "Les Matelots")

But: En somme, un vrai gentilhomme (GOUNOD Faust)

The l in fils is mute, the i is short, and the s is stressed [fis]. The l is normal in the word aile.

Combinations with -il in the middle of a word are always normal when followed by another vowel, as in

milieu, poilu, filial, fusilier, sommelier (but fusiller and sommeiller which are spelled with double l have the ll liquidized).

Au milieu notre barque fuit (LEROUX "Le Nil")

ll is normal in combinations of -all, -ell, -oll, -ull, as in salle, quelle, folle, Lully.

Quelle belle vie! (CHARPENTIER Louise)

A few words with -ill have the normal l. These are ville, mille, tranquille, and their derivatives (see p. 70). *Liquid l and ll.* These sounds have been discussed thoroughly on page 69 in connection with the semivowel [j].

The v and f (ff) sounds. For definition and production see pages 26 and 31. w and ph are pronounced [v] and [f] (as in Wagram, Phidylé). The voiced v is entirely regular and appears in words like voilà, revoir, rêve, etc.

Dites lui qu'il est ma pensée et mon rêve (DUPARC "Au Pays où se fait la guerre")

Je mourrai— mais je veux la revoir (GOUNOD *Roméo et Juliette*)

Voiceless f and ff as an initial or interior sound is always pronounced as in famille, effet, affaire.

Voilà l'*affaire* (MASSENET *Manon*)
Et dans la pieuse *famille* (DEBUSSY *L'Enfant prodigue*)

Final f is also almost always pronounced as in chef, boeuf, oeuf, attentif.

Le mien devient un *chef* fameux (BIZET *Carmen*)
L'air attentif passe sans bruit (MASSENET *Hérodiade*)

f in clef is mute (see also p. 52). In chef d'oeuvre the f is elided. The plurals oeufs and boeufs have the f and s muted.

Voice la *clef*, je crois. (GOUNOD *Faust*)
On ramenait les grands boeufs roux (DEBUSSY *L'Enfant prodigue*)

Cerf and cerfs, appearing in older poetry and music, should also be pronounced with a mute f.

The [z] *sound.* For definition and production of z see pages 25, 32. The voiced s in French can be spelled either s or z.

z is always pronounced initially, as in zèle, zone, Zuniga.

Vous montrez trop de *zèle* (MASSENET *Manon*)
Un *zéphir* vient ternir (WEKERLIN "Bergerettes")

Interior z is also always pronounced, as in bronzé, onzième, gauze.

Azaël, Azaël, pourquoi m'a-tu quittée? (DEBUSSY *L'Enfant prodigue*)
Atteindre ton azur fidèle son beau ciel nacré (SAINT-SAENS "Désir de l'Orient")

Final z is pronounced in gaz and fez. Otherwise it is mute as in voyez, aimez, nez, riz, chez.

Lorsque ses doigts tressent la natte, ou lorsqu' assise auprès du riz (RAVEL "Chansons madécasses")
Voyez-vous toujours en vos songes d'or (CHAUSSON "Amour d'antan")

For the pronunciation of proper names ending in z, like Dumouriez, consult a phonetic dictionary.

Interior s between two vowels of which the first one is not a nasal vowel is pronounced [z], as in visage, raison, résumer, rose, présage, désarmer, réserver, cousin.

Volupté enfin s'aperçu ton visage (HUE "Volupté")
Il pleure sans raison dans ce coeur qui s'écoeuré (DEBUSSY "Il pleure dans mon coeur")
Fâcheux présage (GOUNOD *Faust*)

s followed by a vowel and preceded by a-, anti-, co-, contre-, entre, para-, or pro- is pronounced [s] as in aseptique.

s is voiced [z] in combination with trans-, notwithstanding the nasal vowel, as in transition, transaction, etc., and in Alsace, balsamique Israël.

Israël, romps ta chaîne (SAINT-SAENS *Samson et Dalila*)

s is pronounced [z] before the voiced consonants b, d, g, j, and v, as in sbire, disgrace, disjoindre, and svelte, and in endings on the -isme and -asme.

Les grands jets d'eau sveltes parmi les marbres (FAURE "Claire de lune")

s is pronounced [z] in subsister. s in liaisons is mostly pronounced z (see p. 95).

The s (c, ç) *and* ss *sounds.* For definition and description see page 31.

Initial s is voiceless [s], as in séance, sans, soif.

Partir, nous séparer? Sans doute (BIZET *Carmen*)

But, as mentioned above, when initial s stands before a voiced consonant it changes into [z].

c and sc before e or i are pronounced [s], as in scène, conscience, resusciter, cygne, ceçi, cela.

Ah, cela ne peut être qu'un cierge (CHARPENTIER "La Chanson du chemin")

An intensified [s] should be pronounced in the words transcendant, lascif, rescinder.

Interior s is always pronounced [s] before a consonant other than b, d, g, j, and v, as in lorsque, espérer, distance, estomac.

Mon coeur comme un lys plein s'épanche et je n'ose plus éspérer (DUPARC "Au pays où se fait la guerre")

Lorsque tu parais ange si doux (RAVEL "Chanson des cueilleuses de lentisque")

Interior s or c is pronounced [s] before a vowel if preceded by a consonant as in versez, valsez, arcières. Also in combination with abs-, obs- and subs- (with the exception of subsister) as in obsolète, absolument, subséquent.

Valsez, valsez toujours (GOUNOD *Faust*)

Ce n'est pas là ton dernier mot? Absolumment (BIZET *Carmen*)

Interior s or c is pronounced [s] between two vowels

if the first one is a nasal vowel, as in dansez, linceul, penser, insister.

Sur moi la nuit immense s'étend comme un linceul (BERLIOZ "Sur les lagunes")
J'irai danser la Séguédille (BIZET *Carmen*)

s is pronounced [s] in susurrer.
ç is pronounced [s] as in reçu. ss is always pronounced [s].

Final s is usually mute after a vowel. Exceptions are as (ace), hélas, some names like Pelléas, jadis, fils, lys — but the last is pronounced with mute s in fleur de lis in older poetry; os (in singular form); tous, if used as a pronoun; plus, if followed by que and not preceded by pas or autant, as in La Plus que lente (but: pas plu(s) que lente); plus also if it means the arithmetical term; sens; Saint-Saëns.

Plus in liaison assumes the z sound, as in de plus en plu(s).

Enveloppe-moi du silence argenté des lys (CHAUSSON "Sérénade")
Tes baisers pénètrent jusqu'à l'âme, tes caresses brû-lent tous mes sens (RAVEL "Chansons madécasses")

Final s after a vowel is always pronounced in Greek or Latin words and names: Barrabas, de profundis, Laïs, Thaïs, cosmos, and others.

Final s is always mute if preceded by a mute consonant as in la(cs), me(ts), tem(ps), remor(ds). The sole exception is fi(l)s.

Ah, mon fils (MEYERBEER *Le Prophète*)
Le temps des lilas et le temps des roses (CHAUSSON "Le Temps des lilas")

Final s is also mute if preceded by an r, as in alor(s) and toujour(s), with the exception of the words mars, moeurs, and ours (unless found in old poetry).
s sounds in names of persons and places are pronounced in various ways; consult a dictionary.

The [ʒ] *sound.* This sound is a voiced alveolar-palatal semiocclusive sound which has no equivalent in Italian or German. It corresponds to the s in the English word measure and is produced the same way.

The [ʒ] sound is expressed by the French j or g in the combinations ge, geo, and gi. The [ʒ] never appears as a final sound. Spelled with j it is always followed by a vowel, as in joli, jaloux, ajouter, déjà.

Voulez-vous qu'icy je demeure demi mort tremblant et jaloux (MASSENET "Sérénade de Molière")

Ils ont fui les longs soirs moroses, déjà le jardin parfumé (CHAMINADE "Viens mon bien-aimé")

Spelled with a g in combination with e and i it may be initial, interior, or final, as ir gentil, Geneviève, Gérard, girasol, gymnase, argent, large, mangé, mangeait, ange, rougissant, réagit.

Le cher anneau d'argent que vous m'avez donné (CHAMINADE "L'anneau d'argent")

Un ange est venu dans ma solitude (BEMBERG "Un Ange est venu")

e in combinations of gea and geô is elided, as in vengeance, geôlier (see p. 56).

The ch [ʃ] *sound.* For definition and production see Italian sce, sci, page 35. It must be aspirated somewhat more firmly than its Italian counterpart. This sound corresponds to the English sh. It appears as an initial sound before a vowel, as in chat, chant, chère, chimère, schisme, chaud, chut, chérif, chérubin.

Chère nuit aux clartés sereines (BACHELET "Chère Nuit")

Elle veut de ses *chants* peupler l'air froid des nuits (CHARPENTIER "La Cloche fêlée")

In most words of Greek or Latin origin, the initial ch is pronounced k, as in chaos, choeur, chrétien (see p. 85 for more detailed description).

Choeur [kœːr] immortel! Divine éternelle harmonie (BIZET "Le Matin")

Interior ch is pronounced [ʃ] in French words before a vowel, as in acheter, niche, sécher, échapper, Sancho, Don Quichotte.

Je veux *sécher* tes larmes (SAINT-SAENS *Samson et Dalila*)

In most words of Greek or Latin origin interior ch receives the [k] sound. But words of Greek or Latin derivation keep the [ʃ] sound before a weak e (archevêque, brioche); in some cases before an i; in words with the prefix archi- (archiduc); and in the names Rachel, Michel, Psyché.

Bon Saint *Michel* qui me daignez choisir (RAVEL "Chanson épique")

*Ra*chel, quand du Seigneur (HALEVY *La Juive*)

Je suis jaloux, Psyché, de toute la nature (PALADILHE "Psyché")

Interior ch is pronounced [ʃ] in all words ending in -archie, -machie, -chine, -chique, -chisme, and -chiste, as in machine, catéchisme.

Ch before the consonants l, m, n, and r is always pronounced [k].

Words of Italian origin with ch are pronounced with the [k] sound.

Final ch is very rare. It is pronounced in punch, lunch, tarbouch.

Allumons le punch (OFFENBACH *Les Contes d'Hoffmann*)

The b and bb *sounds.* For definition and production see page 27. bb is always pronounced like a single b. Initial b appears in a multitude of words, such as bête, bal, Bacchus, bière, bruit.

Je suis le spectre d'une rose que tu portais hier au bal (BERLIOZ *Le Spectre de la rose*)

D'aller ainsi dans ce cirque bête (DEBUSSY "Chevaux de bois")

Interior b is always pronounced, be it before a vowel or a consonant, as in robe, tombe, ombre, obstine, absolumment, abbé.

Sous la tombe elle emporte mon âme et mes amours (BERLIOZ "Sur les lagunes")
La seule ombre qu'on ait c'est l'ombre du vautour (CHAUSSON "La Caravane")

Final b is mute in French words and their plurals as in aplomb, plombs.

Final b is pronounced in foreign words and names like club, Jacob, Moab.

The p and pp *sounds.* For definition and production see page 32. pp is pronounced like p. Initial p appears in many words: péril, pas, partir, pleurer, pitié.

O mère du verbe incarné: pitié, pitié! (MASSENET "Souvenez-vous, Vierge Marie")
Entends ma voix chanter, entends ma voix pleurer dans la rosée (FAURE "Chanson Toscane")

Initial p is also pronounced in the ps combination, as in psaume, psychologie, Psyché.

Interior p is always pronounced, be it before a vowel or before a consonant, as in rompre, opportun, applique, symptome.

Et pour fuir la vie importune (DUPARC "Chanson triste")

Qui se répand dans l'air chargé d'ivresse (CHAUSSON "Printemps triste")

Interior p before a t is mute only in the following words: ba(p)tisme (and all derivations of it), se(p)t, se(p)tième (but not in its derivations such as septembre), exem(p)ter (and derivatives except exemption), com(p)te (and its derivatives), prom(p)titude, dom(p)ter (and its derivatives).

Mais ce qui domptait mon esprit (CHAUSSON "Le Charme")

Final p is quite rare and mute in French words such as loup, beaucoup, trop, champs, camp, galop, drap, and their plurals.

In cap, cep, hip, hop, houp, and in foreign words such as stop and group, the p is pronounced.

Final p is mute in the words rom(ps), cor(ps), exem(pt), tem(ps), printem(ps).

Lève toi, lève toi, le printemps vient de naître (BIZET "Chanson d'avril")

Le temps des lilas et le temps des roses ne reviendra plus à ce printemps-ci (CHAUSSON "Le Temps des lilas")

ph is pronounced f (see p. 75).

The d and dd sounds. For definition and production, see page 27. dd, which is very rare, is pronounced like d, as in addition and adition, pronounced alike.

Initial d offers no difficulty. It is pronounced crisply but without any explosion in dans, dormir, doux, depuis.

Mais la vague légère avec son doux refrain (FAURE "Les Matelots")

Depuis le jour (CHARPENTIER *Louise*)

Dans les bois l'amoureux myrtil (BIZET "Vieille Chanson")

Interior d is pronounced before vowels and consonants, as in adosser, jeudi, mademoiselle, rendre, adversaire, adjoindre, admirer, sourde.

Pour rendre le juge propice (FAURE "La Rançon")

Laisse ta mante lourde et ton manchon frieux (BIZET "Chanson d'avril")

J'aime qu'on m'admire (MASSENET "Première Danse")

Final d is mute in all French words and their plurals.

These words usually end in -and, -end, -aud, -oud, -ard, -erd, -ord, and -ourd, as in brigand, défends, chaud, regard, perds, accords, lourd.

Lour*d* d'une tristesse royale (CHAUSSON "L'aveu")
Quan*d* ton regar*d* tomba sur moi (CHAUSSON "Le Charme")

In some words of foreign origin the d is sounded, as in sud, Cid, David.

The t *sound.* For definition and production, see pages 32–33. tt is pronounced like single t.

Initial t or th is always pronounced t decidedly but altogether without explosion, as in tabac, tort, tiens, tu, théâtre.

Qui le *t*ient si longtemps, mon Dieu (DUPARC "Au Pays où se fait la guerre")
Mais ce soir, *t*out a l'heure au *th*éâtre (OFFENBACH Les Contes d'Hoffmann)

Interior t is pronounced [t] before the vowels a, e, o, u, and the nasal vowels, as in détacher, hâter, atone, partout, actualité, attends, rotond.

Me recompensent de l'at*t*ente (DUPARC "Phidylé")
Hâte toi (GOUNOD Faust)

Interior t is pronounced [t] if spelled th, as in sympathie, gothique, etc.

Interior t is pronounced [t] between a vowel and a consonant as in pupitre.

Interior t is pronounced [t] between two consonants, if the second is an r, as in astral. Otherwise, the sequence of three consonants is difficult for a Frenchman to pronounce. The t is therefore usually elided as in as(th)me, is(th)me, etc.

The ti *group.* Interior ti is pronounced [si], except after s as in question, modestie, bestial.

Et quelle modes*tie* (GOUNOD Faust)

The ti in the words étiage, châtier, and chrétien is also pronounced [ti]. These words were spelled with an s in old times (chréstien).

Ti is also pronounced [ti] in the forms of the verb tenir and its composites, as in contient, maintiendrai, soutien.

Je veux un trésor qui les con*tie*nt tous (GOUNOD Faust)
Je te sou*tie*ns de toutes mes forces (POULENC "Nous avons fait la nuit")

Interior ti is pronounced [ti] in the endings on -tions

of verbs, as in étions, partions, chantions, mentions, portiez, mentiez.

Interior ti is pronounced [ti] in the feminine endings of the past participle of verbs ending in -tir, as in partie, sortie.

Elle est partie (GOUNOD Faust)
Et nous étions liés pour toujours ainsi (DEBUSSY "La Chevelure")

Interior ti is pronounced [ti] in the words pitié, moitié, amitié, antienne, sortie, ortie.

Pitié, pitié pour mon martyre (CHAMINADE "Rose-monde")
Dont s'exhale l'humble antienne (DEBUSSY "C'est l'extase langoureuse")

Interior ti is pronounced [ti] in endings on -ique, such as poétique, prophétique; also in adjectives or nouns that end in -tier, -tière, like entier, charcutier, tabatière.

Le monde entier pour se cacher (POULENC "Je n'ai envie que de t'aimer")
Cette tabatière a son secret (LIADOFF "Une tabatière à musique")

The final t sound. Final t with or without the plural s is generally mute, as for example in petit, saint, concerts, meurt.

Mon âme meurt de trop de soleil (DEBUSSY "De Fleurs")
Petit père, petit père (DEBUSSY Pelléas et Mélisande)

In the following words the final t is pronounced: fat, mat, pat; in the Latin words fiat, stabat, vivat; in the word soit, if it stands by itself; and also in net, fait, if the word is accentuated as in au fait (but never when it appears in its plural form); and finally in dot, chut, zut, luth, rut, brut.

Soit: on paiera! (BIZET Carmen)
Mon vieux luth s'éveille (THOMAS Mignon)

Final t is pronounced after the consonants c, p, and s, as in abject, succinct, rapt, abrupt, transept, est (east), ouest.

The final t in the singular verb est (is) is always mute.

Finally, final t is pronounced in the numerals sept (the p is mute; see p. 80) and huit, and their combinations, such as vingt-sept, dix-huit, if they stand by themselves or are not followed by a consonant; the t of vingt is also pronounced by liaison in the number vingt et un.

Le voilà, le beau Vingtunième! (DONIZETTI *La Fille du régiment*)
Elle avait trois lys à la main et sept étoiles dans les cheveux (DEBUSSY *La Damoiselle élue*)

The g sound. For definition and production see page 28. gg is pronounced like single g. Exceptions are the words suggérer, suggéstion, suggéstif, which are pronounced [sygʒere, sygʒestiõ, sygʒestif].

Initial and interior g is pronounced [g] before an a, o, ou, u, [ɑ̃], and [õ] as in galant, agonie, goût, figure, brigand, gonfler.

Je t'adore, brigand! (OFFENBACH *La Périchole*)
Ainsi ton galant t'appelle (GOUNOD *Faust*)

g before e and i is pronounced [ʒ] (see p. 78). Words of Teutonic origin, however, retain the g in French: Gerolstein, Peer Gynt.

Gu before e and i is pronounced [g], as in guérir, guerre, guider, ligue, guitare.

Et les anges venus à notre rencontre chanteront,

s'accompagnent de leurs guitares (DEBUSSY *La Damoiselle élue*)
Que peut-être je guérirai (DUPARC "Chanson triste")

Exceptions are the word arguer, where the u is pronounced [argɥe]; a few words such as aiguë, ambiguë, exiguë where the mute e has the hiatus sign [ɛgɥe]; also in nouns ending in -uité, such as oxiguité.

Words with -gui can also be combinations of g with the semivowel [gɥ] (see pp. 70–71).
Words with -gua are pronounced [gwa], as in alguazil, jaguar.

Initial and interior g is pronounced [g] before all consonants with the exception of n, as in gloire, dogme, grand.

Le long du quai les grands vaisseaux (FAURE "Les Berceaux")
Gloire immortelle de nos aïeux (GOUNOD *Faust*)

Initial and interior g before n is almost always pronounced [ɲ] (see p. 74). There are, however, exceptions. Words of Greek origin with gn, such as gnome, physiognomie, diagnostic, are not liquidized. Also the words stagnant, stagnation, agnat, magnat are not liquidized.

[84]

Magnolia used to be liquidized, but for euphonic reasons it now has the [gn] sound. On the contrary, the words agnus and magnificat, which formerly had the [gn] sound, should be liquidized because of the Pope's ruling about the correct pronunciation of Latin.

Le livre vieux qui se déplie du Magnificat ruisselant (RAVEL "Sainte")

Final g, as in sang, poing, long, longtemps, vingt and derivatives, joug, and doigt, is never pronounced.

Des rivières de sang vont être répandues (BERLIOZ L'Enfance du Christ)

Et son petit doigt coquet relève sa robe (MASSENET "Première Danse")

In foreign words, the final g is pronounced, as in zigzag.

Zig, zig, zag (SAINT-SAENS "Danse macabre")

The k sound. For rules of definition and production see page 34. cc is pronounced [k]. Initial k appears in a very few foreign words, such as képi, kilogramme. Initial [k] is pronounced in words starting with c before the vowels a, o, u, ou, u [ü], [õ], and [œ̃], and all con-sonants, as in carillon, cortège, cueillir, couler, coeur, cuisine, candeur, comte, claque, cric-crac.

où l'on cueille à pleine main (FAURE "Rêve d'amour")

Ils voient couler les ans (DEBUSSY L'Enfant prodigue)

Elle ne croyait pas dans sa candeur naïve (THOMAS Mignon)

Interior [k] follows the same rules, as in reculer, accabler, occasion, Bacchus, aucun, acclamer, éclat, écraser, artistique, ecclésiastique.

qui ne se prend à aucun piège (POULENC "Le Garçon de Liège")

Et sous les fleurs, écrasée (DELIBES Lakmé)

Interior c is pronounced g in the word second and all its derivatives.

ch followed by a, o, u, l, m, n, and r is pronounced k in many words of Greek origin, such as chorus, Chérubini, écho, orchestre, Christ, chrétien (see also p. 79).

De la joie frais échos mêlés au vent qui frissonne (FAURE "Dans les ruines d'une abbaye")

Alors je demanderai au Christ notre Seigneur (DEBUSSY La Damoiselle élue)

Note: ch before the vowel i is sometimes pronounced k as in brachial, orchidée (see also p. 79). For pronunciation of c and sc before e and i, see page 77. cc before e or i is pronounced [ks] as in acceleration, accident.

Acceptez cet air de guitare en échange d'un bon repas (SEMET "Sérénade Gil Blas")

The c in combinations of ct is pronounced [k] as in instinctif, action, tact, direct, respectueux.

Des fous que tu respectes, des simples où tu te baignes (POULENC "Nous avons fait la nuit")

ct is mute in respe(ct), aspe(ct), instin(ct).

Final [k] is pronounced after a vowel other than a nasal one as in lac, sac, cognac, bec, sec, avec, Abimelech, Calpack, Klein Zach, Eisenach. This rule holds true also for the plurals, with the exception of la(cs).

Et j'ai sur le bec . . . un bon coup sec (MONSIGNY Le Roi et le fermier)
Il était une fois à la cour d'Eisenach un petit avorton qui se nommait Klein Zach! (OFFENBACH Les Contes d'Hoffmann)

Final c after a nasal vowel is mute as in banc, flanc, tronc.

Comme ils vont du fer de leur lances harceler le flanc des taureaux! (BIZET Carmen)
Vite, à mon banc de pierre! (MASSENET Manon)

The word donc presents difficulties. It is pronounced [dõk] (with a slight [k]) if it stands at the beginning of a sentence as in "Donc c'est fini"; and also if it is used in the sense of a logical conclusion as in "Je pense, donc je suis," or if it is underlined by stress; also before a vowel, usually tied to it by liaison.

Dieu! où donc est elle? (HALEVY La Juive)

The c in donc is not pronounced before a consonant and at the end of a phrase.

Vous êtes don(c) sorcier? (GOUNOD Faust)
Tu ne m'aimes don(c) plus? (BIZET Carmen)

Words with q are pronounced like [k] as in coq, cinq, inquiet, question, tranquille, Quinquin, quand, que, qualité.

Cinq ans et pas de leçons! (MASSENET "Première Danse")

Sois sage ô ma douleur et tiens-toi plus tranquille (DEBUSSY "Recueillement")

qu is sometimes, but rarely, pronounced [kw], as in quatuor, obséquieux, loquace.

The x sound. The x is a combination of several sounds, its pronunciation depending on the succeeding vowel. Initial x is rare but always pronounced [ks] as in xylophone.

Interior x is pronounced [ks] as in axe, fixer, maxime, extase, exquise, luxe.

C'est l'extase langoureuse (DEBUSSY "C'est l'extase langoureuse")
C'est l'heure exquise (HAHN "L'Heure exquise")

Interior x is pronounced [s] in soixante, dix-sept, Bruxelles.

Interior x is pronounced [z] in deuxième, sixième, dixième, dix-huit, dix-neuf, six heures, deux hommes.

x in the prefix ex, followed by s, ce, or ci is pronounced [k], as in excellent, exciter, excentrique.

Cependant l'excellent docteur Bolonais (DEBUSSY "Fantoches")

x in the prefix ex-, followed by a vowel or a mute h, is pronounced [gz], as in exalter, example, exhaler, exil, existence, exotique, exubérant, exaucer.

S'exalte et se brise comme la mer (D'INDY "Lied maritime")
Comme un prince acclamé revient d'un long exil (DEBUSSY "Voici que le printemps")

In the word execrable, the x is pronounced [ks].
Final x is usually mute, as in deux, doux, faux, aieux, heureux, paix, prix, croix.

Il est doux, il est bon (MASSENET *Hérodiade*)
Aux important la paix (DEBUSSY "Recueillement")
Deux éclats tombés des cieux (DEBUSSY "Fleurs des blés")

The x in six and dix is mute, but it is pronounced [s] before the names of some months, as in six avril, dix octobre, and, for instance, in phrases such as j'en ai six.
Final x is pronounced [ks] in a few words of foreign origin, such as sphinx, lynx, syrinx, lux.

Sphinx étonnant, véritable sirène (MASSENET *Manon*)
Pour le jour des Hyacinthies il m'a donné une syrinx (DEBUSSY "La Flûte de Pan")

The r sound. In pronouncing the French r we encounter the same problems as in Italian or German, with the addition of yet another. The so-called Parisian r is widely used in speech. It is produced by relaxing the tip of the tongue toward the lower teeth, at the same time lifting the back of the tongue toward the palate. In this way, a sound is produced which is not unlike a soft guttural German ch. In singing, however, this Parisian r is never used — at least not by serious interpreters of French vocal art music, because it distorts the vocal line and muddies the enunciation. (For definition and production, also for more detailed discussion of the various r's, see pp. 10–11.) With the Parisian r eliminated, there remain the two other kinds: the dental or rolled r, and the uvular or guttural r. The former is the one mostly used by French singers. It is a common mistake of many English-speaking singers who want to appear more French than the French singers themselves, to employ the Parisian r. The accompanist or coach, however, ought to insist on the dental rolled r.

rr is pronounced like a single [r], but a longer roll on emotionally stressed words with rr, such as terreur, terrible, horreur, erreur, may be excused.

Initial r presents no phonetic problems. It is en-

countered in a multitude of words — rare, rose, rire, rouler, rond, rue.

Et les soirs au balcon voilés de vapeur rose (DEBUSSY "Le Balcon")
Sur votre jeune sein laissez rouler ma tête (DEBUSSY "Green")

Interior r is always pronounced after a vowel and usually also after a consonant as in partir, fermer, glorieux, furieux, mercredi, arracher, courroux, corriger.

Il est à moi! C'est mon esclave. Mes frères craignent son courroux (SAINT-SAENS Samson et Dalila)
Glorieux il se promène avec une allure de prince indien (RAVEL "Le Paon")

r before mute e and after a consonant often tends to be elided or sounded very lightly, as in notre, votre, ordre, être, libre, quatre, maître. But this exception pertains mostly to everyday speech. Composers of songs usually see to it that a separate note is allotted to the syllable -tre of, for instance, no-tre.

No-tre métier, no-tre métier est bon (BIZET Carmen)
Oui, mon maître (OFFENBACH Les Contes d'Hoffmann)

Final r with or without the plural s is regularly pronounced, as in clair, zéphir, amour, trésor, hier, fier, chers, mer, ver, vers, hiver, coeurs, toujours.

Voici l'hiver et son triste cortège (FAURE "Charité")

Je rêve aux étés qui demeurent toujours (FAURE "Ici-bas")

Final r is silent in infinitives of verbs ending in -er, and in nouns and adjectives ending in -ier.

Chante(r), aime(r) sont douces choses (MASSENET Manon)

Viens te coucher(r) sur mon cœur (CHAUSSON "Cantique à l'épouse")

Telle aussi mon âme eut voulu mourir du premie(r) baise(r) (CHAUSSON "Le Colibri")

Cavalie(r) pâle au regard de velours (SAINT-SAENS "La Solitaire")

Final r is also mute in nouns and adjectives ending in -cher or -ger, such as danger, léger, gaucher, rocher.

Oh, que ton jeune amour, ce papillon léger (FAURE "Les Roses d'Ispahan")

Dans mon premier danger je veux dire ton nom (BIZET Carmen)

Final r followed by a mute consonant changes the r from mute to pronounced, as in par(s), per(d), dor(t), cor(ps), bour(g).

Il perd la tête (BIZET Carmen)
Vieux bourgs, jeunes maîtresses (GOUNOD Faust)
Oh, quand je dors (LISZT "Oh, quand je dors")

THE LIAISON

We have arrived at the concluding section about French singing diction; liaisons are the most complex aspect of French singing diction. Except for a few established rules, they are controversial, even among Frenchmen. The evolution of the French language has not bypassed the liaisons; on the contrary, their use is proof that style and taste are in continuous flux. It is no exaggeration to say that liaisons which were made thirty to forty years ago have been abolished and are scoffed at today. My colleagues and I were dumbfounded when the venerable octogenarian conductor Pierre Monteux, an undisputed master of French musical culture, upon returning to the Metropolitan Opera after an absence of nearly forty years, changed a sizable part of the established liaisons in the operas he conducted. It took some time and thought to find the explanation: his way of treating the liaisons evidently represented the style and the taste of his youth, fifty or sixty years before, and was the result of his intimate personal and artistic knowledge of French composers, starting as far back as Massenet.

The style of a performance — as I shall elaborate on later — is the product of three influences: the inherent style of a composition, the taste and musical practice of the age in which it is written, and the taste and practice of the age in which it is performed. This is also true of the practical use of French liaisons. Apart from the few established rules, it is mainly a matter of taste and culture. There is no highest authority to fall back upon. I do not claim to be by any means infallible. All I can do is to make accompanists and coaches conscious of the difficulties and to give them the rules, as well as the logical and esthetical reasons for the treatment of the liaisons in this chapter. Undoubtedly, the deeper the accompanist or coach descends into the well of the French language, the easier he will find it to solve the intricacies of the liaisons.

A liaison is the connection of the final mute consonant of one word and the initial vowel or semivowel or mute h of the following word. Of course, pronounced final consonants are also linked to the following vowel but one does not really call these liaisons. Many more liaisons are made in music and poetry than in everyday language. Rules for liaisons can be divided into three categories: where liaisons must not be made; where liaisons must be made; where a liaison is optional and the handling of it depends upon the taste and preference of the artist or teacher.

Forbidden liaisons. No liaison must be made before an aspirated h.

Que j'admirais de tous mes yeux, les | hameaux, les grands bois, la plaine (MASSENET *Manon*)

Et si je puis braver les | haines sacrilèges de l'ennemi triomphant (DELIBES *Lakmé*)

Liaison is to be avoided between words separated by punctuation marks.

Et tous deux, | oubliant le nom qui les outrage (GOUNOD *Roméo et Juliette*)
Si vous voulez, | amis, on peut la consulter (GOUNOD *Mireille*)

Wherever a liaison could produce misunderstanding of words for grammatical reasons, or where a liaison would change the meaning, it must be avoided.

Dans les lianes posée et sous les fleurs, | écrasée elle attend des gens heureux (DELIBES *Lakmé*)

The word et is never connected by liaison to the following word.

Et | il écoute, point d'alarme dehors (RAVEL "Le Grillon")
Il le vise du bec, et | il plonge tout à coup (RAVEL "Le Cygne")

Liaison must never take place between the words oui, huit (numeral), onze, or the exclamations oh and ah and the final consonant of a preceding word. Dix-huit and vingt-huit never use the liaison.

The mute final consonant of a noun or pronoun in the singular should not be tied over to its verb by liaison except for euphonic or musical reasons — if, for instance, the absence of a liaison would leave two vowels of identical or very similar kind unconnected.

Obéissons, quand leur voix appelle (MASSENET *Manon*)

Without liaison the [wa] and [a] would sound very unpleasant. This rule is to be taken with a grain of salt, anyway. In fast musical declamation, fluency will demand liaisons whether or not they are grammatically correct.

In phrases like mot à mot, nuit et jour, de temps en temps, liaison is made.

Il veille et nuit et jour mon front rêve enflammé (WIDOR "Albaÿde")

Nouns ending in a nasal vowel are not to be connected by liaisons.

Le printemps | est venu, ma belle (BERLIOZ "Villanelle")

Adjectives and adverbs ending in a nasal vowel are tied over by liaison with the exception of chacun, selon, environ, and quelqu'un, which are never tied over.

Chacun | à son gout (JOHANN STRAUSS *Die Fledermaus*)

No liaison should be made between the pronouns ils, elles, and on, placed after the verb in a question, as in sont-elles | arrivées?

Whenever a rest or a hiatus interrupts the flow of the

musical phrase the liaison must not be made unless the tempo is very fast or unless a liaison helps the vocal line (in Figs. 74, 75, and 76 no liaison is made).

Mais, ô mon bien-ai-mé,

Figure 74. Saint-Saëns, *Samson et Dalila*

Voy-ez! quels re-gards et de quel é-clat

Figure 75. Bizet, *Carmen*

Jour et nuit je me mets en quatre, Au moin-dre

Figure 76. Offenbach, *Les Contes d'Hoffmann*

Required liaisons. Most liaisons are made between words belonging to the same phrase in a sentence. There must be some logical or musical connection between the words. If this connection exists, and if none of the rules which prohibit a liaison applies, the words should be linked.

Liaison is made between articles or pronouns such as les, des, ces, un and the following noun or adjective.

Cette rose c'est ton haleine, et ces étoiles sont tes yeux (DEBUSSY "Nuit d'étoiles")
Tout mon bonheur s'est envolé sur les ailes de la fauvette (BIZET "La Vieille Chanson")

Liaison is made between personal pronouns and the verbs to which they belong.

Vous arrivez fort mal (BIZET *Carmen*)
Ils accouraient, nuit et jour (HAHN "Si mes vers avaient des ailes")

Liaison is made between on and tout and the verb to which they belong; also between verbs and the words to which they belong in the question form.

Entre nous, tout est fini! (BIZET *Carmen*)
Et que l'on ait été par vous abandonné (MASSENET "Souvenez-vous, Vierge Marie")

Liaison is made between possessive, indefinite, and qualifying adjectives and the word to which they refer. Also between numerals and the word to which they refer.

Dans nos deux esprits ces miroirs jumeaux (DEBUSSY "La Mort des amants")
Ouvre au matin tes ailes (RAVEL "Chanson de la mariée")

Liaison is made between dont, quand, soit . . . soit, tant . . . que, tout, très, bien, quant à, and the words that follow them.

Soit par hasard soit à dessein (BIZET "La Vieille Chanson")
Quant à toi beau soldat, nous sommes manch(e) à manche (BIZET Carmen)

Liaison is made between prepositions and the words which follow them.

dans un pays lointain (CHAUSSON "Chanson perpétuelle")
Ah, sans amour, sans amour s'en aller sur la mer (FAURÉ "Chanson du pêcheur")

Liaison is usually not made between vers (toward) or hors and the words that follow them except for euphonic reasons.

Pourquoi n'irai-je pas vers elle? (GOUNOD Faust)

Liaison is made between the third person singular or plural of avoir and être and the following word; also between auxiliary verbs and the infinitive which follows.

Les lys ont enfermé leur cœur (MASSENET "Crépuscule")

Il eut en échange un baiser d'adieu (GOUNOD Mireille)

Liaison is made between two adverbs.

Il n'est pas encore mort (GOUNOD Faust)

Optional liaisons. Actually, all liaisons which are not expressly forbidden by the rules can be made, but sometimes taste and understanding require that they should not. In such places liaisons are optional, sometimes doubtful. No rules can be established. Euphony, the musical line, and, last but not least, the period in which the particular piece was composed are the criteria; of course, whatever we choose will be permeated with the taste of our time. In classical French music, liaisons are numerous. In modern music the tendency is toward fewer liaisons, though speed and fluency are conducive to making them.

I shall give but one example to illuminate the problem (Fig. 77). This "Je dis, hélas" has been the subject of

Figure 77. Bizet, Carmen, undesirable liaison

constant discussion among coaches. Partisans of the liaison claim it should be made notwithstanding the comma, because the melodic line requires it. Their adversaries fight against liaison, maintaining that the comma rules it out completely. I side with the latter group, not only because a slight break before the exclamation hélas is helpful to underline Micaela's plea, but also because I think the analogy with the first "Je dis" makes a separation desirable. But I realize that adherents of the unbroken legato line have the right to insist on their way of handling this phrase.

Specific rules for liaison. I have discussed the grammatical, esthetical, and musical rules for liaisons. Now we shall see how the different mute consonants are treated when tied over to the following vowel. In singing, it is extremely important to pronounce consonants tied over by liaison as late as possible and as gently as possible, and to lose only a minimum of time on them before gliding over to the following vowel.

b does not lend itself to a liaison.

Mute c is not tied over, as in blanc et noir.

The adjective franc and the noun porc can be linked to a following vowel.

Mute d of nouns is not likely to be linked by liaison.
Par un grand froid | au bois j'étais seulette (CHARPENTIER "La Petite Frileuse")

d is linked over in inverted verbal forms when the verb comes before its subject, or in adjectives when followed by their qualifying nouns, as in un grand écrivain.

The d of quand is tied by liaison.
Quand il eut achevé (DEBUSSY "La Chevelure")

The d in liaisons of quand, grand, and second is pronounced like a soft t, as in un grand ami ([grɑ̃t ami:]).
Le grand astre torrentiel (CHABRIER "Les Cigales")

In the combination rd the mute d is not apt to be tied over; instead, the r is linked.
Je ne pus d'abor(d) en répondre (CHAUSSON "Le Charme")

No liaisons are made with the f. The word neuf, however, can be tied by liaison. The f in this case is pronounced v, as in neuf heures ([nœv œ:r]). For euphonic reasons one would pronounce neuf enfants ([nœf ɑ̃fɑ̃]).
There is no unanimous opinion about the ability of

the final g to be tied over by liaison. In nineteenth-century music, however, a liaison is preferable, as in sang (h)umain, if not expressly prohibited by one of the above general rules. g in liaison is pronounced like a soft k. The words cing, poing, and seing are not apt to be linked by liaison.

Mute l is not tied over by liaison. The word gentil can be tied over but the l is in that case liquidized. Sonorous final l and liquidized l and ll are, of course, always tied over.

Sous le mol abri de la feuill(e) ombreuse (FAURE "Nell")

Liaison is never made with r.

The nouns ending in -an, -ien, -yen, -in, -ain, -oin, -on, -in cannot be linked to the following vowel.

Que ce vin | est mauvais (GOUNOD *Faust*)

The situation becomes complicated, however, in the case of adjectives, pronouns, prepositions, and adverbs. The words ancien, certain, hautain, humain, lointain, moyen, plein, prochain, soudain, souverain, vain, vilain before a noun are tied over by liaison. But they lose their nasal quality, as in vain espoir ([vɛn ɛspwar]).

De quelque lointain Angélus (CHABRIER "Les Ci-gales")

If the adjective is not followed by a noun the liaison does not take place, as in vain | et faux.

Bien, combien, and rien are apt to be tied over if tied to the following word logically, but they keep their nasal quality.

Nous n'avons rien à nous dire (DEBUSSY "La Flûte de Pan")

Adjectives ending in -in are not denasalized because if they were they would assume the feminine ending -ine. An exception is the word divin.

Oh! Sois béni divin enfant (BERLIOZ "L'Enfance du Christ")

Adjectives ending in -an do not adapt to liaison. En as pronoun, adverb, or preposition is subject to liaison.

Mon, ton, son, bon are tied over by liaison, but are denasalized.

Mon amour quand tu berceras mon triste coeur et mes pensées (DUPARC "Chanson triste")

Mon bonheur renaît sous ton aile (BACHELET "Chère Nuit")

On is subject to liaison without denasalization.

Ce bouquet eut le sort des choses qu'on oublie (MARTY "Fleurs fanées")

Words ending in -un are liable to liaison, but are not denasalized, because they would assume the feminine ending -une.

Sous ta fenêtre un autre chante (CHARPENTIER "A Mules")

Un is not tied by liaison in the phrases: un et trois, un ou deux, un et un. The liaison is made when the noun is multiplied by un, as in vingt et un ans. In the expressions un à un, l'un ou l'autre, l'un avec l'autre, l'un et l'autre, l'un après l'autre, the liaison is optional.

Je les écouté, un à un (HUE "Les Clochettes des muguets")

p does not lend itself to liaison.

For q, see c.

Le coq a chanté (SAINT-SAENS "Danse macabre")

Nouns ending in -er and -ier are not tied over if the following word is an adjective or a verb.

De blé le grenier | est plein (PIERNE "Le Mou-lin")

Adjectives ending in -er, if followed by a noun, are liable to liaison, as in premier ami.

Verbs ending in -er are subject to liaison, especially in music.

In all liaisons, the r must be pronounced very softly, the singer immediately gliding over to the following vowel.

We must distinguish between s as singular ending and the plural s. In almost all liaisons the s is pronounced voiced z.

The singular s. Nouns are usually tied over.

Par ton printemps embaumé (DUVERNOY "Douces Larmes")

Adjectives are also tied over.

Pour que tu sois la plus aimée (PALADILHE "Les Trois Prières")

Verbs are mostly tied over.

Viens‿auprès de ma couche (LISZT "Oh, quand je dors")

Verbs in the second person singular ending on -es are not subject to liaison, as in Tu chantes | à l'opéra.

Some verbal endings of être do not lend themselves well to a liaison, especially those ending in -es or -s, as in Tu as | aimé.

Prepositions like dans, des, sans, chez, sous, après, depuis are linked to the next word.

Après‿un rêve (FAURE "Après un rêve")
Et vais me mirer dans un flot (LALO "La Chanson de l'alouette")

The adverbs plus, moins, très, assez, puis, autrefois, parfois, longtemps and the words pas, plus, jamais are likewise linked over to the next word.

N'est-il plus‿un parfum qui reste (DEBUSSY "Romance")
Qui n'est pas aimé perd le moi de Mai (CHARPENTIER "Prière")

Mais may or may not take the liaison, depending upon punctuation and musical phrasing.

Mais‿en attendant qu'il vienne (BIZET Carmen)

Mais, ô mon bien‿aimé (SAINT-SAENS Samson et Dalila)

ss keeps the [s] sound in liaisons.

The words fils, jadis, lys, which were tied over in former times, now tend to change the [s] sound to [z] in liaisons.

The plural s. Most plural forms are subject to liaison. Where the plural s follows another mute consonant, the s is tied over.

Voyez les! regards‿impudents (BIZET Carmen)

Words in singular form link the r.

Le discour(s)‿est très net (BIZET Carmen)

The verbs (je) pars, (tu) sors, tie over the r. Toujours, hors, vers, envers follow the same principle, as in ver(s)‿un monde meilleur.

Et nous étions liés pour toujour(s)‿ainsi (DEBUSSY "La Chevelure")

In words with plural s a liaison is usually made with the s ([z]), as in plusieurs‿enfants.

Splendeurs‿inconnues, lueurs divines entrevues (FAURE "Après un rêve")

The x is subject to liaison. It assumes the sound [z].

La paix_est faite (GOUNOD *Faust*)
Des bons vieux airs_très connus (MASSENET "Première Danse")

The x in the word noix is never linked.

The z sound, too, is tied over, as in restez_avec moi.

Laissez_un peu, de grâce (GOUNOD *Faust*)

The z in the words nez and riz in the singular is not subject to liaison, as in ne(z) à ne(z); in the plural form it is tied over.

PHONETIC TRANSCRIPTION OF CAVATINA
FROM GOUNOD'S "FAUST"

kɛl trublə̃kɔny: mə penɛːtrə? ʒə sɑ̃ lamuːr sɑ̃pare: də
mɔn‿ɛːtrə! o margəriːtə, a tə pje mə vwasi:!
saly:! dəmoerə ʃast e pyrə, u sə dəviːnə la prezɑ̃ːsə
dyn‿aːm inɔsɑ̃ːt e diviːnə! kə də riʃɛːs ɑ̃ sɛtə povrətɛ:!
ɑ̃ sə redwi:, kə də felisitɛ:! o natyrə, sɛ la kə ty la fi si
belə!

se la kə sɛt‿ɑ̃fɑ̃ a dɔrmi su tɔn‿ɛːl, agrɑ̃di: su tɛz jø.

In endings with ts, the s is linked to the next word.
In general the t is tied over by liaison.
Mais ce que serait cet‿émoi (CHAUSSON "Le Charme")

The conjunction et is never subject to liaison with the following word.

In endings with rt, the r is linked to the next vowel.

De chaque branche par(t) une voix (HAHN "L'Heure exquise")
O sor(t) amer, ô dur(e) absence (BERLIOZ "L'Absence")

The adverb fort ties the t over, as in fort‿aimable. Likewise the t is subject to liaison in interrogative phrases.

For reasons of euphony the t is tied over in:

Cela ne sert à rien (BIZET *Carmen*)

ct endings tie the t over.

In the words aspect, respect, suspect, and circonspect, the c ([k]) is tied over, as in quel aspec(t) affreux. This, however, is an antiquated rule. Today, both c and t tend to be mute.

la kə tɔn alɛːnə ᾶvəlopɛ̃ː sɔn aːmə, ty fiz avɛk‿amuːr
epanuiːr la famœ̃ sɛt‿ᾶ͡ʒə de sjɛl sɛ la! wi, sɛ la!

PHONETIC TRANSCRIPTION OF FAURE'S
"LES BERCEAUX"

lə lɔ̃ː dy keː, lɛ grᾶː veso:, kə la huːl‿ɛ̃nklin ᾶ silᾶsə,
nə prɛnə paː gard‿o bɛrso:, kə la mɛ̃ de famə balᾶsə.
mɛ vjɛ̃dra: lə ʒuːr dɛz‿adjø, kar il fo kə lɛ famə plørø,
e kə lɛz‿ɔme kyriø: tᾶte lɛz‿ɔrizɔ̃: ki lørə!
e sə ʒuːr la lɛ grᾶ veso:, fɥᾶ lə pɔːr ki diminyə, sᾶtə
lør masə rətəny: ə paːr laːmə de lwɛ̃tɛ̃: bɛrso:.

Spanish Phonetics and Diction

As is true of all other European languages, the variety of Spanish dialects is great, extending not only to the frontiers of the Iberian peninsula but to Central and South America as well. The cultured singer of Spanish music will restrict his diction to two main dialects. When he sings songs written in Spain or by Spanish composers and poets he will employ the Castilian pronunciation. When he sings Spanish music from the Western hemisphere he will use a somewhat different pronunciation. And even here, the diction varies: Argentinians or Chileans pronounce certain sounds quite differently from, for instance, Mexicans.

But for all practical singing purposes, the accompanist or coach will have to teach Castilian Spanish and the Mexican variety. The vocal literature used in concerts in the United States is not overly rich. One will encounter principally songs by de Falla, Turina, Obradors, Niñ, and Granados; Mexican songs by Ponce and Revueltas; and the large array of folk songs of Central and South America.

Spanish phonetics differ from their Italian counterpart in only a few respects. I shall therefore limit myself to discussing the sounds characteristic of Spanish. At the end of this chapter I shall transcribe phonetically one Castilian Spanish and one Mexican song.

VOWELS

In singing, all Spanish vowels are pronounced like the Italian vowels. This rule is also valid for vowels which may be pronounced differently in spoken Spanish, such as the a (akin to the French a).

The e and o vowels are usually open, but not quite so open as the Italian [ɛ] and [ɔ]. I shall, however, use these signs in Spanish phonetic transcriptions.

The y when it stands by itself is pronounced like an Italian i.

SEMIVOWELS

Spanish has the [w] and the [j] semivowels. The semivocalic pronunciation is used when i, y, or u stands before a more open vowel.

Cualquiera que el te*j*ado (DE FALLA "Seguidilla murciana")

Voy a partir al p*ue*rto donde se halla la barca (PONCE "Voy a partir")

Clavelitos, que v*ie*nen de Gran*a*da (VALVERDE "Clavelitos")

Yo no sé qué siento (DE FALLA *El amor brujo*)

DIPHTHONGS

Spanish has diphthongs like German. The two vowels need not be sung separately as in Italian, but are connected in a diphthongal sound, as in aire, auto, oiga.

Así que el ba*i*le empie*z*a, si h*ay* don*ai*re (GRANADOS *Goyescas*)

La mi sola, L*au*re*o*la (OBRADORS "La mi sola, Laureola")

Cuando est*oy* a t*ú* lado (MEXICAN FOLKSONG "Yo no sé si me quieres")

CONSONANTS

Consonants that cannot be found in Italian are j, x, z, and b, d, g, in some positions and combinations.

The voiced occlusive sounds b, d, and g keep their occlusive quality as initial consonants, as in *beber*, *decir*, *gato*, and as interior sounds when they are preceded by an m or n, or. in the case of the d, also by an l.

These occlusive sounds change into voiced fricative sounds in so-called weak positions, i.e., as interior sounds. The b (phonetically expressed by [β]) in this case is pronounced as a lazy v, as an American from the South would pronounce it in love. The lips make a slight effort to close, but never quite effect the occlusion.

Y yo, como soy tan po*b*re (NIN "El vito")

Luz de mis ojos, si luz no hu*b*iera, Ha*b*ías de ser (MEXICAN FOLKSONG "Carmela")

D [ð] in an interior (weak) position is a voiced dental fricative produced and pronounced like the th in the in the English words the, other, this, as in lado, desnudo. As final sound, the d becomes very soft and indistinct.

Pue*d*e que en el camino nos encontremos (DE FALLA "Seguidilla murciana")

Interior g [ɣ] before a and o and a consonant other than m or n receives a weak velar fricative voiced sound.

It is produced the same way as the Italian g (see p. 28), but occlusion is not effected. The back part of the tongue and the soft palate never quite connect, as in analogo, luego.

Vivir lejos de tu vega (BARIERA Y CALLEJA "Granadinas")

Desengañémonos ya, mal pagado pensamiento (NIN "Desengañémonos ya")

The g in Spanish can stand for several other sounds as well. Before an e and an i, it becomes a voiceless velar fricative sound similar to the ch [x] in the German ach, or the Scottish loch (see p. 138 for production). The only difference is that the Spanish ge or gi sounds are produced slightly more forward, in the velar section of the mouth, not in the uvular, guttural spot. They are therefore not so explosive or so strongly stressed as their German equivalents.

No se te vaya a escapar y te vaya a ti acoger (OBRADORS "El molondrón")

Olas gigantes que os rompeis bramando (TURINA "Tres poemas")

Más toreo y más gitano (OBRADORS "Canción del café de chinitas")

The gu sound is pronounced [g] before an e or i, or a consonant, and [gw] before an a or o.

Le juyes, y te persigue (DE FALLA El amor brujo) Pregúntale al manso rio (MEXICAN FOLKSONG "Pregúntale á las estrellas")

Acaso al rey del día guarda rencor (GRANADOS Goyescas)

Gü before an e or i is pronounced [gw].

Y hay que ver las coces que le dió mi "agüelo" (OBRADORS "El molondrón")

Spanish y [j] is pronounced like the English y and in you except when it stands by itself (see p. 101). In strong emotion it may become a fricative like the ch in the German ich.

Spanish j in all positions is pronounced [x], as in Juan, hijo, mujer. As final sound it tends to disappear, as in reloj.

A la Jota que hay muchas palomas (NIN "A la jota")

Las azoteas y calles hierven de curioso pueblo, que en él fijando los ojos (TURINA "Romance") qu before an e or i is pronounced [k], as in queso, quedar, quien.

Spanish c before a, o, or u is pronounced [k], as in comer, casa, cuyo.

El *que* las moriscas lunas llevó glorioso a Toledo y torna con mil cautivos y cargado te trofeos (TURINA "Romance")

cu before another vowel is pronounced [kw], as in cue, cui, cuerpo, cuidado.

*Cu*alquiera que el tejado tenga de vidrio (DE FALLA "Seguidilla murciana")
Dame Amor besos sin *cu*ento (OBRADORS "Al amor")

c before an e and i is a voiceless dental fricative [θ], as in cinco, diciembre. It is pronounced like th in thorn, wrath.

Por menos precios se vende (DE FALLA "El paño moruno")
Duérmete, lucerito de la mañana (DE FALLA "Nana")

This is true only of Castilian Spanish. In Mexican Spanish c before e or i is pronounced [s], as in French. Southern Spain – Andalusia in particular, home of the most beautiful folk songs – pronounces c as the French and Mexicans do. It is therefore quite justifiable to sing many of the de Falla, Turina, Granados songs in this way.

ch in Spanish is pronounced like the Italian [tʃ], as in charro, ancho.

Guarda quizás su pe*ch*o oculto tal dolor (GRANADOS *Goyescas*)
Como la man*ch*a oscura orlado en fuego (TURINA "Rima")

Spanish ñ (as in doña, señor) is simply a way of indicating that palatal nasal sound is required. It corresponds to the Italian and French gn [ɲ].

ng and nc (as in ningun, nunca) – [ŋ] – are pronounced as in the German words singen, Anker, or the corresponding English words sing, anchor.

ll (as in llamar, allegar, allí) – [ʎ] – is the Spanish equivalent of the Italian gl. In singing, the ll is pronounced somewhat weaker than in speaking.

Alma sintamos! Ojos *ll*orar! (NIN "Alma sintamos")
"Madre, á la ori*ll*a" (DE FALLA "Canción")

ll in Central America is pronounced like the liqui-dized ll in the French word fille.

Whereas the word llamar in Castilian Spanish is pronounced [ʎama:r], its Mexican pronunciation is [jama:r].

The single Spanish r is produced exactly like the Italian r, and pronounced somewhat more strongly. r between vowels and as a final sound is weak, as in pero, mujer. This last sound is different from the Italian final r, which is always strong.

Initial r, r after an n or s, and rr (as in rosa, garra, arbol, honra) are pronounced very strongly, much stronger than their Italian counterparts.

Antes de que rompa el día (OBRADORS "La madruga")
Arrieros semos (DE FALLA "Seguidilla murciana")

s in Spanish (as in soy, estoy, rosa, más) equals the Italian voiceless s.

Agua quisiera ser luz y alma mía (TURINA "Anhelos")
Soy más valiente que tú (OBRADORS "Canción del café de chinitas")

s before a voiced consonant takes on the voiced sound, as in rasgar [rrazgar].

Spanish z equals the sound of the c ([θ]) before e or i, as in zapato, hizo, diez.

¿Corazón, porque pasais? (OBRADORS "¿Corazón por-que pasais?")
Tres morillas tan lozanas (OBRADORS "Tres morillas")

In American Spanish the z is pronounced like the voiceless Italian s.

Spanish h is silent. Hu before vowels is pronounced [w] as in huelga, huevo.

The Spanish x is pronounced [ks] as in inextinguible, exhalar. In South American Spanish the j sound is now mostly spelled with an x and pronounced [xl], as in Méjico-Mexico.

Many Mexican proper names of Indian origin, such as Xochimilco, Tuxpan, Ixtapan, contain an x. There is no set rule for pronunciation of these names. For in-stance, Xochimilco is pronounced [sɔtʃimilkɔ], Oaxaca [ɔaxaka], Tuxpan [tukspan].

DOUBLE CONSONANTS

All double consonants in Spanish are pronounced strongly and explosively as in Italian. Liaisons and separations in Spanish singing diction are made the same way as in Italian.

PHONETIC TRANSCRIPTION OF MEXICAN SPANISH FOLKSONG: "PREGUNTALE A LAS ESTRELLAS"

preguntale a las estrejas, si nɔ de notʃe me vɛn jɔraːr, preguntale si nɔ buskɔ, para aðɔrarte la sɔleðad. preguntale al mansɔ riɔ si ɛl jantɔ miɔ nɔ ve kɔrrer. preguntale a tɔðɔ ɛl mundɔ si nɔ ɛs prɔfundɔ mi paðeser. ja nunka duðes ke ɔ te kjerɔ, ke pɔr ti mwerɔ lɔkɔ de amɔr; a naðje amas, a naðje kjɛɾes, ojé las kexas de mi amɔr.

preguntale a las flɔres, si mis amɔres lɛs kwentɔ jɔ, kwandɔ la kajaða notʃe sjɛrra su brotʃe, suspiːrɔ jɔ,

preguntale a las aːves, si tu nɔ saːβes lɔ ke ɛs amɔr, preguntale a tɔðɔ ɛl praːðɔ, si nɔ ɛ lutʃaðɔ kɔn mi dɔlɔr. tu bjen kɔmprendes, ke jɔ te kjerɔ, ke pɔr ti mwerɔ, sɔlɔ pɔr ti; pɔrke te kjerɔ bjen de mi viːða, sɔlɔ en ɛl mundɔ te kjerɔ a ti.

PHONETIC TRANSCRIPTION OF CASTILIAN SPANISH: "SEGUIDILLA MURCIANA" FROM THE SEVEN NATIONAL SONGS BY MANUEL DE FALLA

kwalkjera ke ɛl texaðɔ teŋga de viðrjɔ, nɔ deββe tirar pjeðras al del veθinɔ. arrjerɔs semɔs. pweðe ke en ɛl kamiːnɔ nɔs enkɔntremɔs!

pɔr tu mutʃa inkɔnstanθja jɔ te kɔmparɔ kɔn peseta ke kɔrre de manɔ en manɔ; ke al fin se bɔrra, i krejendɔla falsa naðje la tɔma!

German Phonetics and Diction

THOUGH we are confined in Italian and French to tradition and experience as our supreme law for phonetics and diction, we can base our rules for German diction on an officially sanctioned publication, *Deutsche Bühnenaussprache-Hochsprache*, by Theodor Siebs, which was published and republished at the initiative of the Association of German Theatrical Stages and the German Actors Union. It numbers among its contributors the foremost experts in phonetics and stage diction, and deals with singing diction as well. The accompanist or coach who wants to give his pupils an authoritative account will do well to own the book. My experience with German diction has at almost all points been supported by this book. I base this chapter on it and will deviate only where I believe that adjustment to singing diction is necessary.

The vowels in German are, as in the Romance languages, the main elements on which the tones are built. They must be sung clearly, without any trace of diphthongization, unless coloring, covering, or blending of tones into vocal phrases warrants a certain adjustment. In German, as in the Romance languages, the tones are sung on vowels, the consonants following them being drawn to the next vowel. There is a widely held misconception that German is the language of harsh consonants. The old Wagnerian school and some singers of the past, who stressed consonants in a heavy Teutonic fashion have done great harm to the singing of German. As in many other musical fields, our taste has changed here, too. Today we prefer German to be sung according to the principles of the classical Italian school of singing, giving full rights to the onomatopoetical power of consonants, but with the diction based primarily on pure articulation of vowels.

THE A VOWEL

There are only two a's in German, the long a as in Rat and Fahrt, corresponding to the English word father, and the short a as in Mann and Sache, corresponding to the second a in the English exclamation aha!

The long a sound. a in German is long when it is spelled aa or ah, as for instance in Aar, Paar, Saal, Fahrt, Wahn. Phonetically, it is expressed by the symbol [a].

Wahn, *Wahn*, überall *Wahn* (WAGNER *Die Meistersinger von Nürnberg*)
Woher ich kam der *Fahrt* (WAGNER *Lohengrin*)

It is long when it forms the end of a syllable, as in da, ja, Vater, graben, tagen.

Walvater harret dein (WAGNER *Die Walküre*)
Nur hurtig fort, nur frisch gegraben (BEETHOVEN *Fidelio*)

When a stands in front of a single consonant in the same syllable, as in kam, war, Grab, Schwan, it is long.

Nun sei bedankt, mein lieber Schwan! (WAGNER *Lohengrin*)
Ein Stündlein wohl vor Tag (WOLF "Mörike Lieder")

The a in some words to which the above rules appear to apply is short: ab, Ungemach, Walfisch, am, Bräutigam, Garten, hart, das, was, du hast, er hat, Monat, Klatsch.

Wie wehr ich da dem *Ungemach* (WAGNER *Die Meistersinger von Nürnberg*)
Ich muss hier *warten* (RICHARD STRAUSS *Elektra*)

The short a sound. a is short in front of more than one consonant, as in bald, Land, Rast, warten, lassen, and before sch, as in rasch, Fasching.

a before ch and ss is usually short, as in Bach, wachen, nass.

Warte nur balde ruhest du auch (SCHUBERT "Über allen Wipfeln ist Ruh")
Warten *lassen* (RICHARD STRAUSS *Der Rosenkavalier*)

It assumes the long sound, however, in some cases, as in brach, Frass.

Some words to which the rules for short a's apply have the long a. These are exceptions, expressly created by the committee of experts who regulated German pronunciation. Such words are ihr habt, gehabt, Gemach,

Schmach, Jagd, Walstatt, Schicksal, achtsam, Papst, dankbar, Arzt, Art, Heirat.

Erhebe dich, Genossin meiner Schmach (WAGNER *Lohengrin*)
Auf der Walstatt seh'n wir uns wieder (WAGNER *Die Walküre*)
Noch wie mein' Nam' und Art (WAGNER *Lohengrin*)

The e sounds. There are four kinds of e in German: the long closed e, the long more open e, the short open e, and the weak e. All these sounds can be found in the languages discussed above.

The long closed e [e] *sound.* This sound corresponds to the French é, or the e in the English words chaos and chaotic (for description and production see p. 53).

e is long and closed when spelled ee or eh, as in See, fehlen, or when it is itself a syllable.

Angele*hn*t an die *E*pheuwand (WOLF "An eine Aeolsharfe")
Unsere Liebe muss *e*wig beste*hn*! (BRAHMS "Von ewiger Liebe")
Ich such' im Schn*ee* vergebens nach ihrer Tritte Spur (SCHUBERT "Erstarrung")

e is long when it is the last letter of an accentuated syllable, as in Leben, heben, beten.

Was vermeid' ich denn die W*e*ge (SCHUBERT "Der Wegweiser")
O wie s*e*lig seid ihr doch, ihr Frommen (J. S. BACH "Song")

When followed by a single consonant in the same syllable, as in schwer, wer, wem, e is long.

O wüsst ich doch den W*e*g zurück! (BRAHMS "Song")
W*e*r in die Fremde will wandern, *de*r muss mit der Liebsten g*e*hn (WOLF "Heimweh")

e in word forms contracted by elision of another vowel is pronounced long and closed, as in gebt (which comes from gebet).

G*e*bt eu're Eifersucht nur hin, zu werben kommt mir nicht im Sinn (WAGNER *Die Meistersinger von Nürnberg*)

Some e sounds have been declared long and closed by agreement of the committee of experts (see p. 106), such as Krebs, nebst, Erde, Herd, Pferd, werden, Schwert, Erz, stets.

Ein Schwert verhiess mir der Vater (WAGNER *Die Walküre*)
Wes Herd dies auch sei (WAGNER *Die Walküre*)
Die liebe Erde allüberall blüht auf (MAHLER *Das Lied von der Erde*)

The long, more open ä [ɛ] *sound.* This sound corresponds to the French ê (for description and production see p. 51).

ä is long, but more open when it is spelled äh, as in Ähre, Fährte.

Früh, wann die Hähne krähn (WOLF "Das verlassene Mägdlein")
Die Luft ging durch die Felder, die Ähren wogten sacht (SCHUMANN "Mondnacht")

ä is long and more open when it ends a syllable, as in Träne, Täler.

Träne auf Träne dann stürzet hernieder (WOLF "Das verlassene Mägdlein")

When it is followed by a single consonant in the same syllable, as in Bär, spät, ä is also long and more open.

Aus alten Märchen winkt es hervor mit weisser Hand (SCHUMANN "Aus alten Märchen")

ä is also long and more open before a ch or an ss, if closely related or lengthened forms have the long vowel, as in Gespräch, Gefäss.

Drin ein Gefäss voll wundertätigem Segen (WAGNER *Lohengrin*)

Some ä sounds have been established long and more open by agreement (see p. 106), as in Städte, zärtlich, Rätsel.

Beschirmte Städt' und Burgen liess ich bau'n (WAGNER *Lohengrin*)

The short open e sound. This vowel corresponds exactly to the sound in the English bell and held, or the Italian [ɛ] (for description and production see p. 52).

e or ä is short and open when it appears before more than one consonant or before a ch, as in Held, hält, Nächte, schlecht, Bett.

Ich habe keine guten Nächte! (RICHARD STRAUSS *Elektra*)
Behalt ihn, Held! (WAGNER *Götterdämmerung*)

Some exceptions exist: e is short and open in weg, Herzog, Vers, Herz, es, des.

Was drängst du denn so wunderlich, mein Herz, mein Herz? (SCHUBERT "Die Post")
Doch will der Held nicht Herzog sein genannt (WAGNER *Lohengrin*)

The weak e [ə]. The sound corresponds to the French weak e. (For description and production see p. 54.) e is pronounced [ə] in unaccentuated initial, medial, or final syllables, as in *Gerede, Ebene, alle.*

Geh, Geliebter, geh' jetzt! (WOLF *Spanisches Liederbuch*)
Tiefe Stille herrscht im Wasser (SCHUBERT "Meeres Stille")

This weak e appears in many unaccentuated final syllables on -er, -el, -en, -em, as in *jeder, jeden, jedem.* The English-speaking singer has great difficulty in pronouncing these e's weak. Thorough study of the above rule should suffice to remedy this difficulty. The pronunciation of the word sister may also be used to help in explaining.

Although there is no mute e in German (see p. 54), it is sometimes advisable for vocal reasons to interpolate it between two consonants, especially if they are of the

Figure 78. Weber, *Der Freischütz,* German "weak e"

Figure 79. Mozart, *Die Zauberflöte,* German "weak e"

same kind. The singing line may otherwise be in danger of being broken by the harshness of the consonants, as illustrated in Figure 78 (between wohl and lacht) and Figure 79 (between nicht and der).

THE I SOUNDS

There are two kinds of i sounds: the long closed i and the short open i.

The long closed i [i] *sound.* The long closed i corresponds exactly to the English e in me, see, sea. In German the long closed i appears in words like dir, wir, wider, Lid, Nische. It can also be spelled ie, as in die, Miete, Lied, or ih, as in ihr (for description and production see p. 14). In German, as in Italian, it is most important that the tongue is low and grooved while pronouncing an i sound.

Auf *ihrem* Leibrösslein, so we*i*ss w*ie* der Schnee (WOLF "Der Gärtner")
S*ie*h Tamino, *die*se Tränen fl*ie*ssen, Trauter, d*i*r allein! (MOZART *Die Zauberflöte*)

The short open i sound. The short open i corresponds to the English i in words such as tin, in, bin. In German it appears in all words that are not covered by the above rules for the long closed i. That means i is pronounced short if it stands in front of more than one vowel, as in Tisch, Kind, bitte.

Am fr*i*sch geschn*i*ttenen Wanderstab (WOLF "Fussreise")
Des H*i*mmels Segen belohne d*i*ch! (MOZART *Die Entführung aus dem Serail*)

Some words do not conform to the above rules: in vierzehn, vierzig, viertel, the i should be long but has been ruled short (p. 106) (but not in vier and Vierteil).

THE O VOWEL AND Ö UMLAUT

There is a great variety of o and ö sounds in German. Some have equivalents in English.

The long closed o [o] *sound.* For description and production, see page 16. German o is pronounced long and closed when it is the final sound in a syllable as in so, wo; or if the o stands in front of a single consonant, as in rot, holen; and also in some words containing an o followed by a ch or an ss, like hoch or gross, bloss, Stoss. There are, however, comparatively few of these words. This kind of o car also be expressed by oo, as in Moos, or oh as in Lohe.

Wie ich hinaus v*o*r's T*o*r gekommen (WOLF "Auf einer Wanderung")
Ein St*o*ss – und er verstummt! (BEETHOVEN *Fidelio*)
Ein Wälsung wächst dir im Sch*o*ss (WAGNER *Die Walküre*)
Dämmert der Tag? Oder leuchtet die L*o*he? (WAGNER *Götterdämmerung*)

The o in Obst, beobachten, Obacht, Mond, Montag, Ostern, Trost, Kloster is long.
Der M*o*nd steht über dem Berge (BRAHMS "Ständchen")
Ein Kl*o*ster ist zu gut! (RICHARD STRAUSS *Der Rosenkavalier*)

This pure closed o does not exist in the English language, where it is always diphthongized as in no, oh, cold, blow.

The short open o [ɔ] *sound.* For description and production, see pages 15–16. Short open o stands in front of more than one vowel as in kommen, rollen, kosten. Sometimes also before ch or ss, as in doch, Ross, etc. (consult an orthophonic dictionary).

Du holde Kunst (SCHUBERT "An die Musik")
Er kommt, er kommt, o Wonne meiner Brust! (CORNELIUS *Der Barbier von Bagdad*)
Am leuchtenden Sommermorgen (SCHUMANN "Am leuchtenden Sommermorgen")

There are again a few exceptions, where the o instead of being long has been declared short by the above-mentioned committee of experts: ob, Hochzeit, vom, von, Ost, Osten, erloschen, gedroschen.

Nach Osten weithin dehnt sich ein Wald (WAGNER *Die Walküre*)
Und als das Korn gedroschen war (MAHLER "Das irdische Leben")

In English, this short open o is found only in unstressed syllables as, for instance, in omit, or the o sound

in words that start with the prefix pro- (provide is an example).

The accompanist or coach must be careful to correct any tendency on the part of the singer to pronounce the o toward the darkened a, unless the melodic line warrants it.

THE Ö UMLAUT SOUNDS

These sounds, phonetically, stand between o and e. They can be found long and closed, or short and open. They must be formed by protruding, completely rounded lips. For description and production see page 57.

The long closed ö [ø] *sound.* For description and production, see page 57. [ø] must be pronounced like the long closed eu or oeu in French, as in eux or heureux. It has no real equivalent in English. The nearest approximation can be found in the words learn and herb, but these words are produced with a more open sound. In order to approach and reach the sound of [ø], the lips must be completely rounded and close together and the opening of the mouth must be small, until the real long closed ö sound is perfected.

[112]

ö is long and closed when it forms a syllable by itself, as in Öde, or when it is followed by a single consonant, as in Öl and König. Also it is long and closed if it is preceded or followed by an h, as in Höhle and Möhre, or if its singular form contains a long closed o, as in Schösse (Schoss), Stösse (Stoss).

Der öde Tag zum letztenmal! (WAGNER *Tristan und Isolde*)

O König, das kann ich dir nicht sagen! (WAGNER *Tristan und Isolde*)

In einer Höhle hütet er Fafners Hort (WAGNER *Die Walküre*)

Höchstes Vertrau'n hast du mir schon zu danken! (WAGNER *Lohengrin*)

There are a few exceptions where the ö, although followed by more than one consonant, must be pronounced long, as in Gehöft, Behörde, Börse, trösten, Österreich, rösten.

Nun Herr, wess soll ich mich trösten? (BRAHMS *Ein deutsches Requiem*)

Dem Ahnenspiegel Österreichs (RICHARD STRAUSS *Der Rosenkavalier*)

The short open ö [œ] sound. For description and pro-duction, see page 57. Open ö likewise has no equivalent in English; it corresponds to the open eu in the French coeur.

In German, ö is pronounced short and open wherever it stands before more than one consonant, as in Söller or Wölfe, and also before sch as in Frösche, or in front of ch or ss if its singular of the word has a short open o, as in Köche (Koch), Schlösser (Schloss).

Der Herr auf seinem Rösseli sagt zu der Frau im Schlösseli (MAHLER "Um schlimme Kinder artig zu machen")

Löschet sie, immerzu (BRAHMS "Vergebliches Ständchen")

Ein Wölfing kündet dir das! (WAGNER *Die Walküre*)

The following exercise for English-speaking singers might be helpful: the singer should pronounce the word her in English, then go over to pronouncing the same word with a long closed ö in German by protruding and rounding his lips and making the mouth smaller. In this way he would arrive at an approximate pronunciation of the word hören. The opposite should be done if an open ö is desired; the lips should still be protruded and rounded but the mouth should be opened further. In this way we might arrive at the word Hörner. With these exercises, a singer could learn the correct ö sounds in a short time. Some accompanists or coaches mark with *er* the spots in songs and arias which contain ö's. This leaves too much room for misunderstanding. It is always better to make the singer conscious of the right pronunciation by means of the above exercise and the phonetic explanation of what happens to mouth and lips. Of course, the use of a tape recorder will also help to alleviate the troubles of the English-speaking singer.

The u vowel and ü umlaut sounds. For description and production of u, see page 17. No other vowel creates such difficulty for the English-speaking singer. The u sound in English is pronounced farther back in the mouth than the Italian or German u. Besides, in English it is never pure but is always diphthongized to sound like yu or ui.

This is the right way of pronouncing a pure u: the lips must be rounded into a pout, closing them much more than for the o sound while relaxing the throat all the time. The singer should be made conscious of the fact that the u must be pronounced at the very tip of the lips. The lips are rounded into a circle almost as if they were about to gently blow away a light object.

The long closed u [u:] *sound.* For description and production, see page 17. Long closed u stands in open syllables like du; or if the u precedes a single consonant as in Zug, Mus; and if followed by an h as in Schuh; and sometimes before ch and ss, as in Buch and Fuss.

Schuhmacher und Poet dazu (WAGNER *Die Meister-singer von Nürnberg*)
Ein altes Buch, vom Ahn' vermacht (WAGNER *Die Meistersinger von Nürnberg*)

Exceptions agreed upon are flugs and Geburt and words with the prefix ur- (as in Urwald, Urfehde). Also in Schuster, Wust, husten, pusten, Russ.

Vor allem Volk ward Urfehde geschworen (WAGNER *Tristan und Isolde*)
Der Schuster schafft doch stets mir Pein! (WAGNER *Die Meistersinger von Nürnberg*)

The short open u sound. For description and production, see page 61. u is pronounced thus when followed by more than one consonant, as in Brust, Mutter, or by sch, as in Busch, and also when followed by a ch or ss, if related forms have a short vowel, as in Bruch, Bucht, Schuss, muss.

Füllest wieder Busch und Tal (SCHUBERT "An den Mond")
Wann der silberne Mond durch die Gesträuche blinkt Und sein schlummerndes Licht über den Rasen streut Und die Nachtigall flötet, Wandl' ich traurig von Busch zu Busch (BRAHMS "Die Mainacht") Sandvike ist's, genau kenn ich die Bucht (WAGNER Der Fliegende Holländer)

This short open u does not appear in Italian diction. It must be pronounced forward, without the slightest tension of the throat. The lips are again rounded, but slightly more open than in pronouncing the closed long u. The short open u can be illustrated in English by the words put, foot, good, book, provided that every trace of diphthongization is avoided.

THE Ü UMLAUT SOUNDS

For description and production, see page 60. The ü is the same sound as the French u. It should not present any difficulties for singers who have already mastered French phonetics.

There are two kinds of ü's in German: the long, closed ü, and the short, open ü.

The long closed ü [y:] *sound.* This umlaut is pronounced in open syllables or before single consonants, as in Tür, müde, schwül, also before an h as in führen, fühlen. Again before a final ss in süss, or if the root of the word contains a long closed u, as in Füsse (Fuss), büssen (Busse); also before a ch if the root of the word contains a long, closed u, as in Bücher (Buch), Flüche (Fluch).

Ein Büsser ist's (WAGNER *Tannhäuser*)
Ich träumte von bunten Blumen, so wie sie wohl blühen im Mai, Ich träumte von grünen Wiesen (SCHUBERT "Frühlingstraum")
Wird's nicht zu kühl? 's war heut' gar schwül (WAGNER *Die Meistersinger von Nürnberg*)

Exceptions agreed upon by the committee of experts (see p. 106) Brüche, Gerüche, Küche, Sprüche, where the ü is short and open.

Kannst du dein Sprüchlein, so sag' es her! (WAGNER *Die Meistersinger von Nürnberg*)
Was Fein's aus der Küch' (WAGNER *Die Meistersinger von Nürnberg*)

The short open ü [y] sound. This sound is pronounced if the ü stands in front of more than one consonant or before sch or ss, as in stürbe, nüchtern, Glück, rüsten, Büsche, Gelübde, gebürtig.

Doch stürbe nie seine Liebe, wie stürbe dann Tristan seiner Liebe? (WAGNER *Tristan und Isolde*)
Wenn Dein Gelübde dich bindet mir zu schweigen (WAGNER *Parsifal*)
Zu mir, du Gedüft! Ihr Dünste, zu mir! (WAGNER *Das Rheingold*)

There are only a few exceptions, such as düster and wüst, that according to the rules would have the ü short, but are pronounced by agreement with a long closed ü.

Ein wüstes Gesicht wirrt mir wütend den Sinn! (WAGNER *Götterdämmerung*)

THE Y [y] SOUND

The y in German (pronounced ypsilon) in the middle of a word is always pronounced ü. It appears only in words of Greek derivation. There are two y's, analogous to the two ü's. Since there are comparatively few words with y in German operatic or lied literature it might suffice here to mention a few examples.

The y is pronounced a shade higher (approaching the i) than the ü.

Will suchen einen Zypressenhain (SCHUBERT "Die liebe Farbe")
Freude schöner Götterfunken, Tochter aus Elysium (BEETHOVEN Ninth Symphony)
Zurück, Tochter Babylons! (RICHARD STRAUSS *Salome*)

THE DIPHTHONGS

The diphthongs are combinations of two vowels or of umlaut and vowel which in German speech are pronounced as one unit, very much as in English. They require a change of mouth, lip, and tongue position in the very short time that the pronunciation of the diphthong takes. Such a quick change is not in the interest of uninterrupted bel canto singing. If too many changes of positions of the vocal apparatus have to be made — not only within a word, but even within a syllable — the vocal phrase will be broken and the tone will sound unsteady. For this reason, the German diphthongs must be sung differently from the way they are spoken. The first vowel of the diphthong has to be held longer than the

[116]

second. The singer should proceed to the second vowel of the diphthong just before the following consonant or vowel. There is a definite difference between the Italian (Fig. 80) and the German (Fig. 81) way of singing in this respect. Italian has no diphthongs; it gives equal weight and length to each of two successive vowels. On long notes the first part of the diphthong should be held longer; the second part always stays the same: it should be short and pronounced late.

Oh pa-tro mia, mai più, mai più — ti ri-ve-drò!

(mo-i più, mo-i più)

Figure 80. Verdi, Aïda. Italian diphthong

(ma - eI)

Im wun-der-schönen Mo-nat Mai

Figure 81. Schumann, "Im wunderschönen Monat Mai," German diphthong

This rule may completely contradict the old way of German singing which can still often be heard, even from very prominent German singers. But as I have said before, our taste has returned to the uninterrupted, evenly

produced vocal line of the Italian bel canto, modified for each language, but basically unchanged. No principle of clarity of diction need be broken in following this rule. As a matter of fact the ear — and the heart — will comprehend vocal music much more clearly if singing is built on the beauty of an uninterrupted flow of vocal line.

There are only *three different diphthongs* — ai, au, and eu — in German, although different ways of spelling make them seven.

The ai diphthong sounds. The ai diphthong may also be spelled ei, ay, or ey. In speaking or singing, it is not divided into the vowels a and i, but always into a comparatively bright a and a very short, closed e, as in Leib (sung [laːep]). In analyzing the motions of tongue and lips one will find that the singer does not lift the tongue from the a position to the i position, but after reaching the closed e position will slide over to the next consonant or vowel.

Some examples of the ai spelling are Maid, Mai, Saite, Waise. The ei spelling (pronounced exactly the same way) includes such words as Leib, Seite, Weise. The ay and ey spelling, used in older times (some of it can still be found in old editions of vocal scores or lieder anthologies), is now restricted to names of people and places.

The English equivalent for all these diphthongs is the simple i as in life.

There are a few words (Kain, Mosaik) in which the ai is not a diphthong, but belongs to two different syllables. They are hardly ever found in the German vocal literature.

In exclamations or onomatopoetical words – hei; tandaradei; ei; ei; ai, ai – the second vowel is an open i and gets more stress than the a.

Ei, ei, wie fein! (MOZART *Die Zauberflöte*)
Ai, ai, ai, der Dieb! (RICHARD STRAUSS *Ariadne auf Naxos*)
Hei! Siegfried gehört nun der Helm und der Ring! (WAGNER *Siegfried*)

The au diphthong sound. The au diphthong when sung consists of the vowel a, which is open, and a closed but very short o, as in Maus (sung [Ma:os]). The tongue, and especially the lips, move from the a forward to the u, but before reaching it stop at the closed o and slide from it to the next consonant or vowel.

Weck' ich ihn nun *auf?* (WOLF *Spanisches Liederbuch*)
Das Wasser *rauscht,* das Wasser schwoll (SCHUBERT "Der Fischer")
Ich *schau'* dich an, und Wehmut schleicht mir ins Herz hinein (SCHUMANN "Du bist wie eine Blume")

The English equivalent is the diphthong ou or ow, as in house, now.

There are cases in German where for poetical or onamatopoetical reasons the above ao rule should be broken and the a and the u in the diphthong given their full values. If, for instance, the dreaminess of the word Traum is intended to be stressed, the word should be sung Tra-um (with a very closed, not too short u). Or the word raunen, which means something like to mumble secretively, should be sung ra-unen.

Und wie in Traume raunt er das Wort (WAGNER *Götterdämmerung*)
Lieb' und Leid! Und Welt und Traum! (MAHLER *Lieder eines fahrenden Gesellen*)

The inherent musicality of the au diphthong may be illustrated by the fact that in one of the most musical and singable languages, Finnish, the root for the very words for singing and song is laul.

In an exclamation au! (exclamation of pain) the second vowel is a u and therefore receives more stress than the a.

The eu diphthong sounds. The eu sounds may also be spelled äu, occasionally even oi or oy. These diphthongs consist of an open o and a very short, closed ö, as for instance in Treue. Tongue and lips should move from the open o as if they wanted to attain a closed ü (by rounding the lips), but on reaching the closed ö, they should instead slide quickly to the next consonant or vowel.

Auf, auf, mein Herz, mit Freuden nimm wahr, was heut' geschicht! (J. S. BACH "Auf, auf! mein Herz, mit Freuden")

Niederwallen auch die Träume, wie dein Mondlicht durch die Räume (SCHUBERT "Nacht und Träume")

In exclamations like hoi and hoiho, the second vowel is an open i and gets more stress than the o.

Hoiho, Hagen! (WAGNER Götterdämmerung)

Wherever the u after an e or ä belongs to a final syllable, as in Te Deum, Jubiläum, no diphthong ought to be sung.

THE CONSONANTS

Nowhere has there been so much sinning against the musicality of a language than by the exaggeration of the German consonants. Their so-called harshness has been the basis of many a comedian's repertory and the laughingstock of many an audience. It must be said that some of the worst sinners are to be found among the German singers themselves. This came about mostly as a result of the development of the Wagnerian Sprechgesang, the whole old style of overdeclaiming, overplaying poetry. In our time of underplaying (not to be confused with underprojecting), these singers' sounds hurt our ears and create the unfortunate impression that German is ugly. That this is not so can be best realized when one listers to the the great past and present interpreters of lieder like Lotte Lehmann, Elisabeth Schumann, Richard Tauber, Elisabeth Schwarzkopf, Hans Hotter, and Dietrich Fischer-Dieskau. All these singers build their art entirely on diction, using the finest shades for expressing the deepest emotions. Certainly for dramatic effects cruder means must be used, but this is true in any language.

Quite a few languages have been termed "unmusical":

German and Czech because of their accumulation of consonants, English because of its many diphthongs and even triphthongs, Dutch and Hebrew or other Semitic languages because of their abundance of gutturals. I should like to take this occasion to break a lance for the singability of any language. True, the ones richer in vowels will sound more pleasant to our ears, which are generally trained to enjoy the Italian vocal style. But any language can be made to sound beautiful, and who would close his ears to the charms of a Schubert lied, an old English ballad, an aria from Smetana's *The Bartered Bride* in its original language, or a simple Hebrew shepherd's song?

The following discussion of German consonants will, I hope, definitely prove that they are singable and not offensive to the ear.

SINGLE CONSONANTS

The h sound. The h sound is always aspirated at the beginning of a word like halten or Herr, and when it appears in the middle of a word as the first letter of the syllable which forms the root of the word or is derived from it as in behalten, verhindern, Walhall, Johannes, also in some names such as Beethoven (Bethofən).

Behalt' ihn *Held!* (WAGNER *Götterdämmerung*)
Herr, lehre doch mich (BRAHMS *Ein deutsches Requiem*)
Folge mir, Frau! In Wal*hall* wohne mit mir! (WAGNER *Das Rheingold*)
Nero, der Kettenhund (WEBER *Der Freischütz*)

The h in the middle of a word is also aspirated in exclamations like aha, oho, hoiho, hehe, hihihi, and in some words like Ahorn and Uhu.

Haha! Da hätte mein Lied mir was Liebes erblasen! (WAGNER *Siegfried*)
Hoiho! Hagen! (WAGNER *Götterdämmerung*)

In all other cases the h in the middle of a word is mute and used only to elongate the vowel and close it as, for instance, in all words with ah, äh, eh, oh, öh, uh, and üh, such as Fahrt, Fährte, Ehe, sehen, wehe (pronounced [veə]), Lohe ([loə]), Föhre, Ruhe ([ruə]), rühmen.

Ruhe, meine Seele! (RICHARD STRAUSS "Ruhe meine Seele")
Woher du kommst der Fa*hr*t (WAGNER *Lohengrin*)

Wie ein guter Hund auf einer guten Fährte! (RICHARD STRAUSS *Der Rosenkavalier*)

The h after t or r (th, rh) is always mute and does not change the pronunciation of t or r. These forms are relics of the older way of spelling which can still be found in many editions of songs. Needless to say, the th has no relation to the English th. Words with th are Walther and Thron; among words with rh is Rhapsodie.

An h following a p forms the combination of consonants which is pronounced f, as in English.

In strong emotion the h is aspirated with more energy than usual.

du *H*und! (you *dog*!)
*H*immeldonnerwetter! (*H*ell!)

THE VOICED CONSONANTS

As in all other languages, some consonants are singable in German and, indeed, sometimes sung on, thus serving to stress the emotional, poetic, or onomatopoetic possibilities of a word. These consonants can be sustained on musical tones passing through the whole diapason of the human voice. Singable consonants in German are, for all practical purposes, m, n, ng, l, w, s, j, and, to some extent, r.

The m sound. For description and production, see page 22. m may be initial, medial, or final. It is sung exactly as an Italian m would be, whether it is connected with vowels or other consonants. The m must be finished without being exploded, otherwise we should get the effect of a double m as in the Italian word mamma, where this explosive action is indicated. If, however, the m is the final sound of a word as in kam, it may sometimes be right to stress it by adding a mute e (see p. 110); otherwise the m may be lost. But this device should be used only where absolutely necessary (in big theaters or concert halls, where the necessity for projection may dictate it). Final m followed by an initial m will usually be connected without explosion and will sound like the single m as, for instance, in Am Montag, Komm morgen, nimm mich hin.

Ein *M*ägdlein sass a*m* *M*eerestrand (BRAHMS "Treue Liebe")

Du *m*eine Seele, du *m*ein Herz, du *m*eine Wonn', o du *m*ein Schmerz! (SCHUMANN "Widmung")

Die Nacht war kau*m* verblühet (FRANZ "Sonntag")
Mein Held, *m*ein Retter, nim*m m*ich hin! (WAGNER *Lohengrin*)

In some bel canto phrases where it is essential that the vocal line from one vowel to the other must not be disturbed it is necessary to pronounce a very weak m. For further description and examples, see page 22.

The n sound. For description and production, see page 23. n may be an initial, medial, or final consonant. For initial n's or n's between two vowels the pronunciation is the same as in Italian, but care should be taken not to exaggerate it, and the tongue should not be released explosively.

For final n's the same rules should be followed as for the final m. It may sometimes be necessary to explode the final n, adding a mute e, in order to stress the sound adequately.

Leise flehe*n* mei*n*e Lieder durch die *N*acht zu dir (SCHUBERT "Ständchen")
Fleuch', *N*achtigall, i*n* grüne Finster*n*isse, i*n*s Hain-gesträuch (BRAHMS "An die Nachtigall")
Dann flieht der Schlaf vo*n n*euem dieses Lager (BRAHMS "An die Nachtigall")

If n comes before another consonant, especially before m, f, p, b, k, or g, the singer must first complete the n, and then continue to the next consonant, as in a*n*merken, sa*n*ft, a*n*prangen, u*n*brauchbar, u*n*klar, a*n*ge-nehm.

Von Liebe sa*n*ft bedeckt! (BRAHMS "O wüsst ich doch den Weg zurück")
Rosendüfte wehen in dieser dumpfen Felsenkluft (SCHUBERT "Ave Maria")
Bei dem a*n*genehmsten Wetter singen alle Vögelein (WOLF "Der Scholar")
So stolz, so keck, so schade*n*froh (SCHUBERT "Die böse Farbe")

The ng [ŋ] sound. For description and production, see page 24. The effect of this sound is to mold n and g into one sound, as in ju*ng*, stre*ng*, la*ng*, Ju*ng*gesell. The g must not be audible as a separate sound.

O liebliche Wa*ng*en ihr macht mir Verla*ng*en (BRAHMS "O liebliche Wangen")
Ein Ju*ng*gesell muss es sein (WAGNER *Die Meister-singer von Nürnberg*)
Ich hör meinen Schatz, den Hammer er schwi*ng*et (BRAHMS "Der Schmied")

The ng sound does not change if it stands in the middle of a word, as in jünger, jüngst, strenger, länger, Engel, Finger, singen. In English, the g is pronounced in many similar words; in German, it is always unpronounced. The accompanist or coach must see to it that this rule is strictly observed, otherwise the result will be a diction which is not German.

The [ŋ] sound is also used when a single n stands in front of a final k as in Dank ([daŋk]), sink, funkeln.

Und mit ge*sen*ktem Haupte erwartet sie träumend die Nacht (SCHUMANN "Die Lotosblume")
O *sink* hernieder, Nacht der Liebe! (WAGNER *Tristan und Isolde*)
Eine Mühle seh' ich bli*n*ken (SCHUBERT "Halt!")
Habe *Dank*! (RICHARD STRAUSS "Zueignung")

When an n is followed by a g and a full-voiced vowel, as in Ungarn, the g is pronounced in addition to the ng as in [ungarn], (but not in [un-gern]). In this case, the pronunciation of Ungarn is about the same as in the English longer.

The so-called Bayreuth tradition of pronouncing Ring like rink is probably based on a momentary whim of Richard Wagner's during rehearsal and should be disregarded by today's accompanists and coaches.

The ng sound must not be confused with the French nasal an, on, or en sounds where the n is nothing but a nasal resonance sound (see p. 74).

The l sound. For description and production, see page 24. German l is pronounced forward, like the Italian and French l. It can appear as an initial, medial, and or final sound, as in Liebe, kalt, Röslein, Veilchen, Wahl.

Ich *liebe* dich, so wie du mich (BEETHOVEN "Ich liebe dich")
Ein Veilchen auf der Wiese stand (MOZART "Das Veilchen")
Ja ja, ein Meister meiner Wahl (WAGNER *Die Meistersinger von Nürnberg*)

Whether the l precedes a vowel or a consonant or a group of consonants, it must always be pronounced forward and be stressed fully before the tongue continues to the next sound, as for instance in Hälfte and Halstuch.

Helft mir, ihr Schwestern! (SCHUMANN "Helft mir, ihr Schwestern")

The l can be exploded very easily and therefore serves as the main consonant to demonstrate rhythms (tra la la, la la la, or fa la la). Depending on the length or shortness of tone required, the l should be sung on (lall-lall-lall) or passed over (la-lla-lla). But each new initial l must be exploded freshly in the above rhythmical phrases (See Fig. 82, 83.)

Figure 82. Mozart, Die Zauberflöte

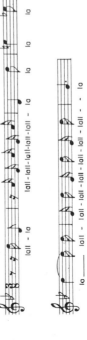

Figure 83. Wolf, Der Corregidor

The w [v] sound. For description and production, see page 25. w in German is akin to the Italian, French,

and English v. It must vibrate and not be similar to the voiceless f where air is simply blown or exploded.

The w is always pronounced the same way whether it is an initial (wahr, Wort) or medial (gewöhnen, schwarz, Schwefel) sound.

Wahn, Wahn, überall Wahn! (WAGNER *Die Meister-singer von Nürnberg*)
Wir wandelten, wir zwei zusammen (BRAHMS "Wir wandelten")
Ein Tännlein grünet wo, wer weiss, im Walde (WOLF "Denk'es, o Seele!")

It can be more or less accentuated, according to the lyrical or dramatical impact of the word.

Some words of foreign origin written with an initial v are pronounced like w, as in vehement, Violine, etc.

Gibt gar nichts auf der Welt, was mich so enflammiert und also vehement verjüngt (RICHARD STRAUSS *Der Rosenkavalier*)
Victoria, Victoria! Der Meister soll leben! (WEBER *Der Freischütz*)

Final w in some names which end on ow (of slavic etymology) is mute; this is true in Bülow ([bylo]) and Flotow.

[124]

The voiced s [z] *sound.* For description and production, see pages 26–27. German s can be voiced or voiceless. The voiced s is used (1) if it is an initial sound, as in Sand, Segen, so, Salome, Sachs; (2) if it appears between vowels in the middle of a word, as in Rose, Hase, Husar; (3) if it appears between an m, n, l, or r on one side and a vowel on the other side, or after a prefix as in Amsel, unser, Ab-sicht; (4) when a word ends with -sal or -sam, as in Schicksal, langsam.

Wir sassen so traulich beisammen (SCHUBERT "Trä-nenregen")

Seltsam ist Juanas Weise (WOLF *Spanisches Lieder-buch*)

Hieher Maid, in uns're Macht! (WAGNER *Das Rhein-gold*)

Many German dialects, especially the southern ones like the Austrian and the Bavarian, do not use the voiced s where it is indicated by the above rules. For this reason, one can hear famous singers "mispronounce" langssam, Ssalome, etc. The accompanist or coach should stress the above rules to the English-speaking singer. Words derived from Greek or Latin have the initial soft s. The voiced s sound is not too pleasant musically if overstressed. Therefore, it should always be sung softly and the tongue should not remain in the voiced s position any longer than is required for clear diction.

The j sound. The j in German is a voiced palatal fricative sound produced by curving the sides of the tongue upward so that they touch the hard palate lightly. The tip of the tongue is curled downward and anchors itself against the ridge of the lower teeth. It corresponds to the English y in you, yore, yard, yes. In German the j is used mostly as an initial sound as in ja, Jahr, jeder, Jugend.

Mein Lieb ist ein Jäger (BRAHMS "Der Jäger")

Von Jasmin und weissen Lilien sollt ihr mein Grab bereiten (WOLF *Spanisches Liederbuch*)

Alljährlich naht vom Himmel eine Taube (WAGNER *Lohengrin*)

It is important to pronounce the j as one consonant and not as a semivowel or semiconsonant (see p. 18).

The gn [ɲ] *and ll* [ʎ] *combinations.* When a German pronounces a French, Italian, or Spanish proper name the [ɲ] and the [ʎ] combinations are pronounced exactly as in their original languages (see pp. 24, 25, 103). Examples: Sevilla, Brogni, Cagliostro, Doña.

The r sound. The r is one of the most important and interesting sounds in German singing diction. It can make the language unnecessarily harsh, if overstressed, or mushy if not projected enough. Different German-speaking regions have different kinds of r's which the singer born in a particular region can change only with the utmost patience and energy. For description and production of the different r's see pages 29–30 and 87–88.

We differentiate in German between a rolled and a flipped r. The rolled r is produced in the throat by the tongue held loosely in low position. This r may be rolled once or more often, until it approaches a throaty trill. The more it is rolled, the harsher the sound will become. The flipped r is the kind used in British English. It is recommended in most cases, because it will present fewer difficulties to the English-speaking singer than the rolled r.

The accompanist and coach must train his charges to forget entirely about the American r except in the endings discussed below.

Vocally speaking, the r has a very important function. It facilitates interval leaps and connection of vocal positions as the neutral gear in an automobile facilitates smooth shifting. It enables the singer to shift from one position into the other without mishap. Because of its voiced quality it will not interrupt the vocal line and will guarantee smoothness of execution.

Und die Treu', 's war nur ein Wort (BRAHMS "Sapphische Ode")
Brich entzwei, mein armes Herze (J. S. BACH "Brich entzwei, mein armes Herze")
Nach Frankreich zogen zwei Grenadier', die waren in Russland gefangen (SCHUMANN "Die beiden Grenadiere")

The r requires very little breath. Because of this, singers will find it convenient to relax on the r for a split second when singing long phrases. The r must be sung clearly, even if successive or consecutive consonants require a rapid shifting of tongue and lip positions, as in Forst, Marktschreier, etc.

Von Hetze und Harst einst kehrten wir heim (WAGNER *Die Walküre*)
Mich dürstet! (WAGNER *Götterdämmerung*)
Der Markt beginnt, die Glocke schallt (FLOTOW *Martha*)

rh in German words (as in Rheingold) is pronounced like a normal r.

Words ending in -er, -em, -en and -el. These unaccented final syllables require special mention because there is so much confusion about them in the minds of English-speaking singers. They think, for instance, that German diction necessitates a very hard pronunciation of the -er endings, with the result that the words sound more Russian than German. The unaccented final syllables all have a weak e ([ə]). The r in the -er combinations is equivalent to the American r, as in sister or better. No flipping or rolling must be permitted. Words with these endings are very numerous: a few are Leder, besser, länger, Wunder.

Tät'st besser, das Leder zu strecken (WAGNER *Die Meistersinger von Nürnberg*)
O hehrstes Wunder! (WAGNER *Die Walküre*)

This rule is also valid for the unaccented final syllable of the first part of a composite word, as in wunderbar, Wasserstrahl, etc.

The weak e (ə) must also be sung in the corresponding unaccentuated syllables on em, en. and el.

Guten Abend, mein Schatz, guten Abend, mein Kind! (BRAHMS "Vergebliches Ständchen")
Wie, welchen Handel hätt' ich geschlossen? (WAGNER *Das Rheingold*)
Ewige Freude wird über ihrem Haupte sein (BRAHMS *Ein deutsches Requiem*)

The b sound. For description and production, see page 27. Initial b's of words or syllables are sung with a slight explosion which will bring out the voiced quality of the b, as in Baum, bergen, Bild, Liebe, Stube.

Wo in Bergen du dich birgst (WAGNER *Die Walküre*)
Es grünet ein Nussbaum vor dem Haus, duftig, luftig breitet er blättrig die Äste aus (SCHUMANN "Der Nussbaum")
Bedeckt mich mit Blumen, ich sterbe vor Liebe! (WOLF *Spanisches Liederbuch*)

The b has only the slightest amount of voicedness and is pronounced very softly at the end of a syllable ending in -lich, -lein, -ling, -nis, -sam, -sal, as in lieblich, Knäblein, Erlebnis, Labsal.

O liebliche Wangen, ihr macht mir Verlangen! (BRAHMS "O liebliche Wangen")

Als Büblein klein an der Mutter Brust (NICOLAI *Die lustigen Weiber von Windsor*).
Der Mutter Erde lass' das ein Labsal sein! (WAGNER *Götterdämmerung*)
Schau, wie das Knäblein sündelos frei spielet auf der Jungfrau Schoss! (WOLF "Auf ein altes Bild")

The b becomes voiceless, hard, and aspirated and approximates a p between a long vowel and a consonant in the same syllable as in gie*bst*, Ob*st*, le*bt*, lie*bt*.

Doch ihr setzet alles auf das jüngende Obst (WAGNER *Das Rheingold*)
Die Lilie soll klingend hauchen ein Lied von der Liebsten mein (SCHUMANN "Dichterliebe")
Und die einsame Träne be*bt* (BRAHMS "Die Mainacht")

The b in e*bn*en and ü*bl*er is voiced and soft. These words in the old spelling contained an e (e*bn*en, ü*bl*er).

Final b is always voiceless, hard, and aspirated if it appears at the end of a word or a syllable. There are, however, two shades of aspiration to be considered.

First: after a long vowel or after r or l, the b approximates a p, which means that the aspiration or explosion is moderately strong, as in Gra*b*, stir*b*, hal*b*.

Mein Lie*b* ist ein Jäger (BRAHMS "Der Jäger")
Denn solchem grossen Sarge gebührt ein grosses Gra*b* (SCHUMANN "Dichterliebe")

Second: after a short vowel, the b is always pronounced explosively and aspirated exactly like a p, such as in a*b*, o*b*, Tra*b*, also in a*b*nehmen, a*b*fahren, and also in the word A*b*t.

Bergab gleitet der Weg (SCHUBERT "An Schwager Kronos")
Rassle den schallenden Tra*b*! (SCHUBERT "An Schwager Kronos")

It is important to remember that the final b in German differs sharply from the final b in English which is sung soft and voiced. The German final b is always voiceless, hard, and must be pronounced like a p.

The d sound. For description and production, see page 27. Initial d (in words or syllables) is always voiced, as in du, da, die, doch, reden, Flieder. It is sung with a more or less strong explosion, depending on the meaning or the accent of the word, but it must always be voiced; otherwise it would sound like a t.

Du *d*a, Loge! sag' ohne Lug (WAGNER *Das Rheingold*)

Wie duftet doch der Flieder (WOLF *Die Meister-singer von Nürnberg*)

The d is almost voiceless, but soft at the end of a syllable before endings on -lich, -lein, -ling, -nis, -bar, -sam, such as in freundlich, Rädlein, Fremdling, ver-wundbar, friedsam.

In ein freundliches Städtchen tret' ich ein (WOLF "Auf einer Wanderung")
Wie friedsam treuer Sitten getrost in Tat und Werk (WAGNER *Die Meistersinger von Nürnberg*)
Doch endlich ward dem Diebe die Zeit zu lang (SCHU-BERT "Die Forelle")

The d is voiceless, hard, and aspirated between a vowel and a consonant in the same syllable, approximat-ing a t, as in du ludst.

The d is voiceless, hard, and explosive at the end of a word or a syllable. This can happen either after a long vowel as in Rad, or after a short vowel plus r, l, m, n, as in Wald, Hemd, Hand.

The final d approximates a t. The aspiration or ex-plosion is moderately strong, as for example in Bad, Fädchen, Lied.

Du denkst mit einem Fädchen mich zu fangen (WOLF "Du denkst mit einem Fädchen mich zu fan-gen")
Meine Laute hab ich gehängt an die Wand, hab sie umschlungen mit einem grünen Band (SCHUBERT "Pause")
So ward es uns verhiessen (WAGNER *Parsifal*)

In such cases the d *approximates* the t: it is not quite the same as the t, which is exploded much more strongly, but it must be completely voiceless.

The d in words like Wandrer, handle, wandle, Redner, and Adler is voiced and soft. The reason for this is the elimination of an e in the modern spelling of the words. (The earlier spellings were Wanderer, handele, and so forth.)

Wandrer nenn= mich die Welt (WAGNER *Siegfried*)
Ihr Edlen mögt in diesen Worten lesen (WAGNER *Tannhäuser*)

It is important to remember that the final d in German differs sharply from the final d in English, which is sung soft and voiced. The German final d is always hard and voiceless and must be pronounced like a t.

The g sound. For description and production, see page 28. Initial g is sung with a more or less slight explosion, the degree of which depends upon the intensity or the accent of the word, as in Gabe, legen, Geliebter, gleich, gegangen.

Dem Vater grauset's, er reitet geschwind (SCHUBERT "Erlkönig")

Gibt das Geleit der Geliebten nach Haus (BRAHMS "Von ewiger Liebe")

Care has to be taken to make the singer conscious of the voiced quality of the g; otherwise it would sound like a k.

g is always soft and voiced at the end of a syllable before the endings -lich, -lein, -ling, -nis, -bar, -sam, as in möglich, Vöglein, Feigling, Wagnis, unsagbar.

Mit Näglein besteckt (BRAHMS "Wiegenlied")

Dank, liebes Vöglein, für deinen Rat! (WAGNER *Siegfried*)

For ng ([ŋ]) before the above endings, see page 123 (as in langsam [laŋza:m]).

The g becomes voiceless and hard between a vowel and a consonant in the same syllable approximating a k, as in regt, liegst, logst, beugt.

Was doch heut Nacht ein Sturm gewesen, bis erst der Morgen sich geregt! (WOLF "Begegnung")

The g is voiceless, hard, and explosive at the end of a word or a syllable. This may happen either after a long vowel or after a short vowel and an r or l. The g then sounds like a k and must be sung aspirated (explosive) and strong, as in Tag, lag, Betrug, Berg, Balg, Burg.

Die Ähren wogten sacht (SCHUMANN "Mondnacht")

Ein Stündlein wohl vor Tag (WOLF "Ein Stündlein wohl vor Tag")

Betrug auch hier! Mein die Hälfte! (WAGNER *Tristan und Isolde*)

The g in words like segnen, leugnen, or in names like Pogner, Pegnitz, Wagner, is *voiced and soft*. The reason for this is again that in earlier centuries these words were written with an e (Wagener), which was eliminated later as the language developed. The same is true for final ge, when the e is replaced by an apostrophe, as in Gefolg', Geheg', leg'.

[130]

[131]

An der Pegnitz hiess der Hans (WAGNER *Die Meister-singer von Nürnberg*)

Freund Pogners Wort Genüge tut (WAGNER *Die Meistersinger von Nürnberg*)

Zeig' her, 's ist gut (WAGNER *Die Meistersinger von Nürnberg*)

Leg' dich zu Bett (WAGNER *Die Meistersinger von Nürnberg*)

Special rules for endings on -ig. If a word or a syllable ends in -ig, or if the syllable is followed by a consonant, the g is pronounced like a soft ch [ç] (see pronunciation of ch on p. 137), as in König, ewig, freudig, Traurigkeit.

Und neu besänftigt wallt mein Blut (BEETHOVEN *Fidelio*)

Helft mir, ihr Schwestern, helft mir verscheuchen eine törichte Bangigkeit, dass ich mit klarem Aug' ihn empfange, ihn, die Quelle der Freudigkeit (SCHUMANN "Helft mir, ihr Schwestern")

Traurigkeit ward mir zum Lose (MOZART *Die Entführung aus dem Serail*)

O König, das kann ich dir nicht sagen (WAGNER *Tristan und Isolde*)

If another soft ch appears in the same word, the ig,

for euphonic reasons, retains its original pronunciation, as in Königreich.

Und wär's die Hälfte meines Königreichs! (RICHARD STRAUSS *Salome*)

It is a rule in German stage pronunciation to soften the g in words with poetical apostrophes, as in ew'ge, sel'ge, etc. In these cases the ge is pronounced like the semivowel [j], as in [evjə], [zeljə]. I do not, however, recommend following this rule in singing diction. It would weaken the vocal intensity.

Ew'ge ([evgə]) Götter! (WAGNER *Lohengrin*)

Den sel'gen Göttern, wie gehts? (WAGNER *Das Rheingold*)

It is important to remember that the final g in German differs sharply from the final g in English which is sung soft and voiced. The German final g is always hard and voiceless and must be pronounced like a k.

THE VOICELESS CONSONANTS

The voiceless consonants, especially when at the end of a word, create a problem for the English-speaking singer which the accompanist and coach can easily solve.

He must impress on the singer that these final consonants must be pronounced absolutely voicelessly, that they have nothing to do with an actual singing tone but are exploded after the vocal sound has come to an end. This will give the singer a welcome opportunity to get rid of his residual breath, since it can be used for the projection of the p, t, k, f, s, etc., or their combinations. Words for which the above is true are knapp, schlappt, klappt, Tat, Stück, Takt, Saft.

Seht hier, wie's schlappt und überall klappt! (WAGNER *Die Meistersinger von Nürnberg*)

Luft, Luft! Ich ersticke! (WAGNER *Tristan und Isolde*)

Glück das mir verblieb (KORNGOLD *Die tote Stadt*)

The p sound. For description and production, see page 32. p can be an initial, medial, or final sound; the pronunciation remains the same. There is not much difference between the English and the German p except that the latter is exploded somewhat more strongly.

Von der Strasse her ein Posthorn klingt (SCHUBERT "Die Post")

Das knospet und quillt und duftet und blüht (BRAHMS "Es liebt sich so lieblich im Lenze")

The t sound. For description and production see page 32. The sound may also be spelled th or dt, as in Thron, Stadt. The pronunciation stays the same. It does not make any difference whether the t, th, or dt is initial, medial, or final. The t sound is almost identical with the English t, except that it must be sung with more intensity and stronger explosion.

Am fernen Horizonte erscheint, wie ein Nebelbild, die Stadt mit ihren Türmen, in Abenddämm'rung gehüllt (SCHUBERT "Die Stadt")

Heb' auf dein blondes Haupt und schlafe nicht (WOLF *Italienisches Liederbuch*)

Thüringens Fürsten, Landgraf Herrmann, Heil! (WAGNER *Tannhäuser*)

The k sound. For description and production see page 34. k can appear in different spellings and combinations, such as ck, x (k+s), chs (k+s), qu (k+w). The pronunciation always stays the same, whether the different spellings of the k are initial, medial, or final.

The k sound is almost identical with the English k, c, ck, qu, and ch sounds, except that it must be sung with more intensity and stronger explosion. In some places of strong emotion, the k, in German, can be aspirated in such a way that an h may be audible after it.

Verwittert Stein und Kreuz', die Kränze alt (BRAHMS "Auf dem Kirchhofe")

Es klingen und singen die Wellen des Frühlings wohl über mir; und seh' ich so kecke Gesellen, die Tränen im Auge mir schwellen (SCHUMANN "Frühlingsfahrt")

Ich will dem Kind nur den Kopf abhaun! (WAGNER Siegfried)

Locket nicht mit Liebesgaben (WOLF "Verborgenheit")

An der Quelle sass der Knabe (SCHUBERT "Der Jüngling am Bache")

qu in German is not related to the semivowel qu in Italian. It is a [kv] combination.

k before n, as in Knabe, must be pronounced, unlike English where it is mute.

The f and v sounds. For description and production see page 31. f and v are pronounced alike, as in Feind, Vater, Veilchen, Frevel, schlafen, brav. Concerning the pronunciation of the v like w in some words of foreign origin, see page 124.

Ein Veilchen auf der Wiese stand (MOZART "Das Veilchen")

Bin Freund und komme nicht zu strafen. Sei guten Muts! ich bin nicht wild, sollst sanft in meinem Armen schlafen (SCHUBERT "Der Tod und das Mädchen")

Zu spät kam ich, und kehre nun heim, des flücht'gen Frevlers Spur im eig'nen Haus zu erspäh'n! (WAGNER Die Walküre)

Der Herr Graf sind auf und davon (RICHARD STRAUSS Der Rosenkavalier)

The v in David and Eva is sung like f, although about ninety per cent of German singers pronounce it mistakenly as w ([v]) (this is southern German dialect). The f may also be spelled ph in some words of foreign origin (Photo, Symphonie). The pronunciation stays the same whether the f, v, or ph appears as the initial, medial, or final sound. The f sounds are almost identical with the English f, gh (as in enough), or ph sounds, except that they must be sung with more intensity and explosion of air.

The pf combination. The pf combination warrants a special paragraph since its execution is very difficult for English-speaking singers. The lips must first be closed tightly for the p, then the upper teeth must come down for the f sound. The p must be aspirated, but the explosion of air takes place only after the f sound as in Pferd, Apfel, Kopf. The singer should be taught to be very conscious of both sounds, first by pronouncing them separately p . . . f, then by combining them in a slow and gradually increasing speed.

At the right tempo one will observe that the lower lip curls inward right after the p has been pronounced so that the upper teeth encounter the lip in place for the aspiration.

Gold'ne *Apfel* wachsen in ihrem Garten (WAGNER *Das Rheingold*)
Mit Näglein besteckt, schlüp*f* unter die Deck' (BRAHMS "Wiegenlied")

The voiceless s sound. For description and production see page 31. Its English equivalent is the s or c (as in race). The difference between the voiced and the voiceless s is the same as between the words buzz and hiss.

The voiceless s in German may also be spelled β especially in the older spelling and after a long vowel, but there is no difference in the way of pronouncing it.

The voiceless s is pronounced (1) at the end of a word or a syllable, as in das, Haus, Häus-chen, loskommen, etc.; (2) when the spelling β is used, as in Fuß, Muße, mäßig, grüßen; (3) in the middle of a word after consonants other than r, l, m, and n, as in Erbse, sechse, rülpsen. The pronunciation does not change whether the voiceless s stands at the beginning, the middle, or the end of a word. The singer should be warned not to explode it too vehemently, otherwise an ugly hissing sound would result.

Knusper, Knusper, Knäuschen, wer knuspert mir am Häuschen? (HUMPERDINCK *Hänsel und Gretel*)
Eine Straße muss ich gehen, die noch keiner ging zurück (SCHUBERT "Der Wegweiser")
Sechse treffen, sieben äffen! (WEBER *Der Freischütz*)

Words derived from Italian and French have the initial voiceless s, as in Santa, Sire, etc.; but if the word has lost its relation to a foreign language, the initial s becomes voiced, as in Sankt ([zaŋkt]).

Jährlich am Sankt Johanristag (WAGNER *Die Meister-singer von Nürnberg*)
Sankta Justizia, ich möchte rasen! (LORTZING *Zar und Zimmermann*)

The st *and* sp *combinations.* Whenever an st or sp appears in the middle or at the end of a word, it is pronounced as written. st and sp, as in bester, hasten, Leiste, Gast, Ost, Wespe, lispeln.

st and sp at the beginning of a word or after a prefix is pronounced sht and shp ([ʃt, ʃp]). See page 136.

The z *or* c [ts] *combinations.* The German z is phonetically a combination of t and voiceless s. It can either stand by itself, as in Zahn, Zeit, Scherz, spazieren, Mozart, or may be spelled ts (after a long vowel) or tz (after a short vowel), as in Rätsel, putzen, Satz, Schatz, Trotz. The German z and c bear no relation to their Italian, French, or English counterparts.

Erklär dies Rätsel, täusch' mich nicht! (MOZART *Die Zauberflöte*)
Guten Abend mein Schatz, guten Abend mein Kind! (BRAHMS "Vergebliches Ständchen")

The c is a combination of tse, tsa, tsee, and appears only in words of foreign origin, as for instance in ecce [ɛktsɛ], Cäsar [tsɛːzar], Citrone [tsitroːnə]. [ts] is produced by bringing into contact the forward part of the tongue and the hard palate, well back of the upper gum ridge. Aspiration or explosion, as in all other consonant combinations in German, takes place after the second consonant. In connecting final and initial z, both must follow the above rule, as in Herz zerstach.

Der jubelnd er das Herz zerstach! (WAGNER *Tann-häuser*)

The x [ks] *sound.* The x is phonetically a combination of k and voiceless s. It may also be spelled chs. It is produced by a fast shift of the tongue from the first to the second consonant, the aspiration or explosion taking place after the s. Some words spelled with x or chs are Axt, Hexe, sechs, Luchs. For general problems arising from the enunciation of voiceless final consonants in singing diction, see pages 132–133.

The sch [ʃ] *sound.* For description and production see page 35. The English equivalent of sch is sh; the sch should therefore present no difficulties to the English-speaking singer. Words with sch are numerous: Schatz, Schule, Esche, rasch, Fisch.

Ich hör meinen *Schatz* (BRAHMS "Der Schmied")

Mit *Schmiegen* und Wenden mir *schlüpft's* an die Brust (WOLF "Erstes Liebeslied eines Mädchens")

Welch' ein Strahl bricht aus der *Esche* Stamm! (WAGNER *Die Walküre*)

In einem Bächlein helle, da *schoss* in froher Eil, die *launische* Forelle vorüber wie ein Pfeil (SCHUBERT "Die Forelle")

Wandl' ich traurig von Bu*sch* zu Bu*sch* (BRAHMS "Die Mainacht")

s with the diminutive ending -chen is not fused into sch, but remains a voiceless, hard s, as in Häus-chen, Füss-chen.

Knusper, Knusper Knäuschen, wer knuspert mir am Häuschen? (HUMPERDINCK *Hänsel und Gretel*)

The initial st[ʃt] *and* sp[ʃp] *combinations.* These sound combinations are pronounced like the English sht and shp. This also holds true for st and sp after a prefix, as in Stolz, Stand, an-stehen, Spott, spassig, ausspielen. The aspiration or explosion takes place after the t or the p, respectively.

Ein *Stoss*—und er ver*stummt*! (BEETHOVEN *Fidelio*)

In ein freundliches *Städtchen* tret' ich ein, in den *Strassen* liegt roter Abendschein (WOLF "Auf einer Wanderung")

Treibe nur mit Lieben *Spott*, Geliebte mein (WOLF *Spanisches Liederbuch*)

Ver*sprochen*? nein das geht zu weit! (BEETHOVEN *Fidelio*)

Initial st and sp in foreign words is pronounced [t, ʃp] only if the word has become part of the German language, as in Spanien (ʃpa:nɛn), Statue (ʃta:tuə).

Als wären Sie die *Statue* auf Ihrer eig'nen Gruft (RICHARD STRAUSS *Ariadne auf Naxos*)

Und keine *spanische* Tuerei! (RICHARD STRAUSS *Der Rosenkavalier*)

st and sp within a foreign word are always pronounced st and sp, as in Restaurant, Aspekt, konspirieren.

The soft voiced [ʒ] and [dʒ] (pronounced in English zh or dzh) appear only in foreign words spelled with g in French, as in genie ([ʒeni:]), or with the g in Italian, as in adagio ([ada:dʒɔ]) or with g or j in English, as in gentlemen or jazz.

The tsch [tʃ] *sound.* For description and production see page 33. This sound is not a combination of consonants but a genuine single consonant which appears in the middle or at the end of German words such as lutschen, hätscheln, Kutsche, etsch. It corresponds to the English ch, as in *church*, or tch as in *fetch*, *hitch*. It is produced and sung just like its English equivalent, or the Italian cia-, ce-, ci-.

Klatscht der Regen auf die Blätter, sing' ich so für mich allein (WOLF "Der Scholar")
Ich peitsche die Wellen mit mächtigem Schlag (SCHUBERT "Der Schiffer")

In singing diction even words with t as the final sound and sch as the initial sound of a syllable are pronounced [tʃ], as in Botschaft, rechtschaffen.

The two ch *sounds*. I have left until last these ch sounds, which cause the English-speaking singer considerable difficulty. Singing them is not, however, an entirely hopeless undertaking. The accompanist or coach can correct faulty pronunciation by insisting that the singer find the position in his speech apparatus where these sounds must be produced.

The ch sounds are not combinations of consonants but regular single consonants, although they differ greatly from each other.

The soft ch [ç] *sound*. The soft ch is a palatal voiceless fricative, produced like its voiced counterpart, the j (see p. 125), except that air is aspirated — but not exploded too violently. There is no English equivalent of this palatal ch. The singer should practice it by saying h as in hue and suddenly aspirating the h until it becomes a soft ch. The resulting sound will approximate very closely the palatal ch of the German.

Soft palatal ch is pronounced whenever ch stands after ä, e, i, ö, ü, ai, ei, äu, eu, as in Bächlein, sprechen, Licht, höchstes, flüchtig, Reich, feucht.

Ich hört' ein Bächlein rauschen (SCHUBERT "Wohin")

Höchstes Vertrau'n hast du mir schon zu danken (WAGNER *Lohengrin*)
In ein mildes, blaues Licht (RICHARD STRAUSS "Traum durch die Dämmerung")
Nun schuf mich Gott zum reichen Mann (WAGNER *Die Meistersinger von Nürnberg*)

Soft ch is pronounced after an l, r, n, as in welcher, Storch, mancher.

Da klappern die Störche im lustigsten Ton (WOLF "Storchenbotschaft")

Redet so viel und so mancherlei (BRAHMS "Von ewiger Liebe")
Denn solchem grossen Sarge gebührt ein grosses Grab (SCHUMANN "Dichterliebe")

Soft ch is also used in the diminutive ending -chen, as in Häns-chen, Mäus-chen, Lüft-chen.

Hänschen klein geht allein in die weite Welt hinein (German folk song)
Wehe Lüftchen, lind und lieblich (BRAHMS "Botschaft")

The ig ending is pronounced like the soft palatal ch (see p. 131).

In some words of Greek or Teutonic origin the initial ch is soft and palatal, as in China, Chemie; but this will hardly ever be encountered in songs or operatic literature.

The hard ch [x] *sound.* The hard ch is a uvular voiceless fricative produced in the throat by anchoring the tip of the tongue against the lower gum ridge and rubbing the back part of the tongue against the back of the soft palate. This guttural ch which is usually transcribed kh in English corresponds very closely to the Scottish ch as in loch. The ch in German is pronounced gutturally whenever it stands after an a, o, u, or au, as in brach, Loch, hoch, Fluch, Rauch.

Ich musste auch hinunter mit meinem Wanderstab. Hinunter und immer weiter, und immer dem Bache nach (SCHUBERT "Wohin")
So will mir doch die ganze Woche das Lachen nicht vergeh'n (BRAHMS "Sonntag")
Wie durch Fluch er mir geriet, verflucht sei dieser Ring! (WAGNER *Das Rheingold*)

The combination chs is pronounced ks, as in wachsen, sechs, Ochs (see p. 135).

Initial ch in foreign words is mostly pronounced like a k, as in Cherubin, Chloë, Christus, Chor.

Ich war bei Chloën ganz allein (BEETHOVEN "Der Kuss")
Edler Täufer! *Christs* Vorläufer! (WAGNER *Die Meistersinger von Nürnberg*)

THE DOUBLE CONSONANTS

The following double consonants exist in the German language:

Voiced	Voiceless
mm bb	ff pp
nn dd	ss tt
ll gg	kk (ck)
rr	

Him - mel, nimm des Don - kes Zäh - ren für dies Pfand der Hoff - nung an!__

Figure 84. Weber, Der Freischütz

Heil dir, Son - ne!

Figure 85. Wagner, Siegfried

Dich, theu - re Hal - - le, grüss' ich wie - der,

Figure 86. Wagner, Tannhäuser

O Herr!

Figure 87. Beethoven, Fidelio

Siebs urges that double consonants be pronounced exactly like single ones. He considers double consonants to be only orthographically, not phonetically, different from their single counterparts. The rule then would be the same as for the pronunciation of French double consonants. This may be valid for stage pronunciation, but we will find that it is too simple to be useful for German singing diction.

One thing is certain: the vowel before a double consonant is invariably a short open one. This distinguishes German pronunciation from the pronunciation of Romance languages (see p. 36), where closed vowels stay closed even before a double consonant. Voiced double consonants similar to the Italian ones give more intensity, impetus, and importance to the words which contain them. This may be illustrated by a few examples (Figs. 84–87). The double consonants in the accompanying list must be sung with much greater intensity than their single counterparts. In a two-syllable word the vowel of the first syllable gets the full tonal value. The double consonant is pronounced and sung at the beginning of the second syllable.

Single	Double
Single	*Double*
Himbeere	Himmel
sondern	Sonne
Halm	Halle
heran	Herr
Rebell	Ebbe
Widmung	Widder
bald	Ball

Figures 84–87 should suffice to make the point that voiced double consonants in German can make the words containing them more expressive, and that they should therefore be more accentuated than single consonants — particularly when dramatic situations or poetic alliterations require special stress. In Figure 84, the invocation of heaven will become more intense if the voice, after scaling the very difficult i sound on a high note, underlines the mm. The same feeling of grandeur and dignity will be achieved by emphasizing the nn in Figure 85, Brünnhilde's invocation of the sun, her first words after her awakening. Jubilation and inner excitement will carry Elisabeth's entrance in Figure 86 if the soprano gives impetus to the double ll in Halle.

In Figure 87, the stressing of the double rr in Herr will convey to the audience the mixture of emotions in Rocco's plea to Pizarro not to command him to murder the imprisoned Florestan. It is a deeply felt pleading, a feeling of impotence to resist Pizarro, and even a suppressed outcry of rebellion against him — all expressed in the one rr.

This is one of the many times when technical and interpretative problems overlap. Siebs had only the technical side of diction in mind when he concluded that single and double consonants should be pronounced alike. To be sure, double consonants must not be overstressed, with the effect of caricaturing the language. The accompanist and coach will have to show the singer the golden middle road of esthetic taste.

THE VOICELESS DOUBLE CONSONANTS

The voiceless double consonants are not much different from the voiceless single consonants. However, a longer pause between forming and exploding the consonant while diminishing the flow of breath (see p. 36) and a somewhat more violent explosion whenever the music asks for it will help to underline the innate drama of words containing double consonants (Fig. 88).

Figure 88. Richard Strauss, "Ständchen," example of voiceless double consonants

Auch der Küsse Duft mich wie noch nie berückte, die ich nachts vom Strauch deiner Lippen pflückte (BRAHMS "Sapphische Ode")

One word about double consonants before other consonants, as in Schlepptau, Schiffsnetz. In such cases the explosion or aspiration of the double consonant is diminished first and intensified only on the last consonant of the group. About the singing of double consonants which belong to different syllables of a word, as in kom-men, ren-nen, bak-ken, see page 139. Although we form the consonant at the end of the preceding syllable it never must be exploded or intensified until we come to the second syllable (Fig. 89, 90).

Figure 89. Mozart, Die Entführung aus dem Serail

Figure 90. Weber, Der Freischütz

COMBINATION OF CONSONANTS

Some combinations of consonants create difficulties for the English-speaking singer, perhaps more for psychological reasons than for technical ones. The most common of these combinations is the *sts*, as in er ist's. The English-speaking singer is prone to disregard pronunciation of the final s, forgetting that there are scores of words in English that contain the same combination of consonants, such as lists and beasts. In all cases of conglomeration of consonants with ts it is advisable to practice singing the preceding consonants, then adding the voiceless ts with the residue of the breath. Some words containing these combinations are Er is-ts, nich-ts, mach-ts, durchziehen, vier-zig, sech-zig, lock-ts, Exzess (but furchtsam with voiced s).

Frühling, ja du bisr's! (WOLF "Er ist's")
Mein Brusttuch, schau, wohl liegt's im Ort (WAGNER Die Meistersinger von Nürnberg)

Wer glaubts? und meiner ward es nicht auf dieser ganzen Reise (SCHUBERT "Der greise Kopf")

Other difficult combinations containing st and sp are, for instance, verstreut, versprochen, durchsprechen, durchstreifen. In these last two, the palatal ch should first be established before tongue and lips continue to the str and spr.

Versprochen? nein das geht zu weit! (BEETHOVEN *Fidelio*)
Einsam zu Ross, ohne Ruh' noch Rast, durchstreift' er als Wand'rer die Welt (WAGNER *Götterdämmerung*)

Other difficulties with combinations of consonants may also be surmounted by first dividing them into two or more units, establishing correct pronunciation for each of them in turn, and then combining them.

CONNECTION OF CONSONANTS

Two or more consonants of the same or of different phonetic groups may have to be connected for musical reasons between two words, or inside the same word, unless they are separated by musical pauses. Certain empiric rules exist. Knowing them will make the work of accompanists and coaches much easier.

Final and initial consonants of the same kind (homorganic) may be found in one word, or in two words, such as in Auf-führung, Schiff-fahrt, Still-leben, hin-neigen, viel lieben, auf Flügeln. These homorganic consonants are, of course, not double consonants. They are connected by pronouncing the final one, then reducing the aspiration during a split-second pause, and then intensifying the aspiration with the start of the following initial aspiration.

Auf *Fl*ügeln des Gesanges (MENDELSSOHN "Auf Flügeln des Gesanges")
Die Stadt mit ihren Türmen, in Aben*d-d*ämm'rung gehüllt (SCHUBERT "Die Stadt")
Und wüssten's die Blumen, die kleinen, wie tief *ver*-wundet mein Herz (SCHUMANN "Dichterliebe")
Wie bitter sin*d d*er Trennung Leiden! (MOZART *Die Zauberflöte*)

The final consonant may be voiceless, the initial one voiced, as in aus-sehen, Bass singen, auf-wenden. Connect these consonants by pronouncing the first one voicelessly, releasing the flow of voice on the second one.

Similar but not homorganic consonants must *not* be connected, as in aus-streuen, aus-sprechen. Each consonant must be pronounced clearly.

Special importance must be given to the connection of final and initial plosive sounds and final plosive sounds with initial consonants of different phonetic classifications. Into the first category fall the t-t, d-d, t-d, d-t, b-b, b-p, b-d, b-g, b-k, b-t, k-d, k-k, k-g, k-t, t-b, t-p, t-g, t-k, g-b, g-d, g-g, g-k, g-p, g-t connections. These and other similar connections are encountered very frequently in vocal literature.

Ihr hoher Zweck zeigt *d*eutlich an (MOZART *Die Zauberflöte*)

Mein Schatz ha*t k*ein Ban*d* und kein Stern (SCHUMANN "Die Soldatenbraut")

Wie Frühlingsblumen blüh*t* es, und schwebt wie Duf*t* dahin (BRAHMS "Wie Melodien zieht es mir")

Sein frevler Mun*d t*at es kund (WAGNER *Tannhäuser*)

Gedenk' *d*er beschildeten Frau! (WAGNER *Götterdämmerung*)

Dem nur in Maienwonne *d*ie zarte Kos*t g*edeiht (WOLF "Citronenfalter im April")

In all these cases connection is effected by keeping the plosive position for final and initial consonants, not ex-

ploding the final sound, concentrating on the consonant during the little pause, and exploding the following initial sound well.

The same rule of exploding only the second sound is valid for connecting final plosive sounds and initial consonants of a different phonetic category. These connections may take place between the following consonants: b-f, b-l, b-n, b-m, b-s, b-w, t-f, t-j, t-l, t-m, t-n, t-r, t-w, g-f, g-j, g-l, g-m, g-n, g-r, g-s, g-w, as in abfahren, ablehnen, Abwege, entfernen, entlehnen, entwöhnen, wegfahren, wegnehmen, Wegweiser, etc.

Frühling lässt sein blaues Band (WOLF "Er ist's")

Doch an andres denk*t m*ein Herz (WOLF *Spanisches Liederbuch*)

Ins Land hina*b*zublicken, das nebelleich*t* zerinnt (SCHUBERT "Der Alpenjäger")

Ich weiss ja doch, du liebtest, allein du lieb*st nicht* mehr! (BRAHMS "Du sprichst, dass ich mich täuschte")

Initial voiced consonants ought to keep their voiced quality to some extent.

LIAISON AND SEPARATION

The glottal stroke. The liaison in German singing diction was taboo in Wagnerian and early post-Wagnerian times. According to my tenet, however, that the German language can be made to sound more beautiful by following a vocal bel canto line, liaisons are permissible and often even preferable.

When the separation of words becomes essential, the English-speaking singer and especially the American and English voice teacher resists using the so-called glottal stroke. Glottal stroke is a violent compression of the vocal cords which explosively releases the stored-up air. Such a glottal stroke is to be used for certain types of violent attack of tones which start with a vowel. This sounds very dangerous and indeed is, if overdone. There are, however, two kinds of glottal strokes: (1) The vehement one, which should never be used because it can actually hurt a voice and create hoarseness by thickening the vocal cords and, in extreme cases, even developing nodes on the vocal cords. (2) The gentle one, which will never hurt a singer who has enough vocal technique to be prepared for professional work on concert or operatic stage.

As a matter of fact, gentle glottal strokes are regularly employed in any kind of staccato singing. There are several situations in which final consonants and initial vowels or one and the same final and initial vowel must be separated: (1) if a word must be isolated for euphonic reasons; (2) if rhythmic or dramatic emphasis warrants it; (3) for clarity of diction, especially in lieder or choral works or passages; (4) to avoid misunderstanding words.

The artist who studies lieder is more likely to use slight glottal strokes than the singer of classical German operatic music. The lied is built entirely on the word. Each shade, be it as soft as can be, must be brought out. The music must paint, color, and embellish the word. Therefore, slight separation between words is essential, unless the vocal line demands an unbroken legato. In Wagnerian operas more glottal strokes are warranted for alliteration and dramatic emphasis than in other German operas. However, his feeling for vocal line will have to guide the accompanist and coach. I cannot warn strongly enough against chopping up phrases and melodies for the sake of exaggerating the misunderstood German diction.

Choral works or passages, because of the masses of voices that are employed in them, will tend to become and separation on the same lyrics. Here the melodic line asks for liaison in accordance with the same phrase at the beginning of this aria: Und ob die Wolke sie verhülle. The legato is indicated by the violoncello melody during the introduction (Fig. 92). In the next line the musical phrasing asks for separation.

In the example from *Lohengrin* (Fig. 93), the words mein and Ohr must be separated; otherwise, the senseless connection "nohr" would result. The same happens in the phrases "mein/Aug' ist zugefallen" and "sank/in süssen Schlaf."

Detailed analysis of the liaison-versus-separation fight would fill a whole book. The above-cited rules and examples will have to suffice. The accompanist and coach must have enough cultural and musical background and knowledge of style — in other words, artistic taste — to decide in each case which approach to use.

PHONETIC TRANSCRIPTION OF GERMAN ARIA: "ELSA'S DREAM" FROM "LOHENGRIN" BY RICHARD WAGNER

ainza:m in tryban ta:gən ha:p iç tsu: gɔtt gəflet, das hertsəns ti:fstəs kla:gən ergɔss iç im gəbet, da: draŋ aus

Sein Au - ge, e - wig rein und klar, nimmt mei-ner

auch mit Lie - be wahr,

Figure 91. Weber, Der Freischütz

sein — Au - ge e - wig rein und klar, nimmt

Figure 92 Weber, Der Freischütz

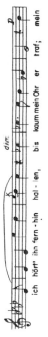

ich hört' ihn fern-hin hal-len, bis kaum mein Ohr er traf; mein

Lento

Aug' ist zu - ge - fa - len, ich sank in sü - ssen Schla.

Figure 93. Wagner, Lohengrin

muddy if the diction is not very clear. Here the separation of consonants and vowels is an important part of choral technique. In Agathe's cavatine from *Der Freischütz* (Fig. 91) we can prove the necessity for a liaison

"WOHIN?" BY FRANZ SCHUBERT

iç hørt ain bɛçlain rauʃen vol aus dem fɛlzənkvɛll, hinap tsum taːle rauʃen zo friʃ unt vundərhɛll. iç vais niçt viː miːr vurdə, niçt, ver den raːt miːr gaːp, iç musstə aux hinunter mit mainəm vandərʃtaːp. hinunter unt immər vaitər, unt immər dem baxə naːx, unt immər friʃər rauʃtə unt immər hɛllər der bax.

ist dass dɛnn maine ʃtraːssə? o bɛçlain ʃpriç, vohiːn? duː hast mit dainəm rauʃen miːr gants bərauʃt den zinn. vas zaːg iç dɛnn vɔm rauʃen? das kann kain rauʃen zain; ɛs ziŋən vol diː niksen tiːf untən iːrən rain.

las ziŋen, gezɛll, las rauʃen, unt vandre frøliç naːx! ɛs gen ja mylənrɛːdər in jedəm klaːrən bax.

mainəm ʃtenən ain laut zo klaːgəfɔll, der tsuː gəvaltgəm tønən vait in diː lyftə ʃvɔll. iç hørt iːn fɛrnhiːn hallən, bis kaum main or er traːf; main aug ist tsuːgəfallən, iç zaŋk in zyssən ʃlaːf.

in liçtər vaffən ʃainə, ain rittər naːtə daː; zo tuːgənt-liçər rainə iç kainən nox ɛrzaː. ain gɔldən hɔrn tsur hyftən, gəlenət auf zain ʃvert, zo traːt er aus dən lyftən tsuː miːr; der rɛkkə vert. mit tsyçtigəm gəbaːrən gaːp trøstuŋ er miːr ain, das rittərs vill iç vaːrən, er zɔll main ʃtraitər zain!

hørt, vas dem gɔttgəzantən iç biːtə fyr gəveːr, in maines faːtərs landən diː kronə traːgə er, miç glykkliç zɔll er praizən nimmt er main guːt dahiːn, vill er gəmaːl miç haissən, geb iç iːm, vas iç bin!

INDEX

Index

q sound, French, 86, 96
qu sound: Italian, 34, 133; French, 86; Spanish, 103; English, 132; German, 132–133

r: 7; Italian, 26, 29–30, 87, 104; American English, 29, 126, 127; English, 29, 126; French, 48, 52, 53, 54, 57, 58, 60, 61, 87–89, 96; German, 87, 110, 121, 125, 126–127, 138, 140; Spanish, 104
"La Rançon" (Fauré), 81
Ravel, Maurice Joseph, 51, 52, 60, 63, 67, 69, 70, 75, 76, 77, 78, 79, 85, 88, 91, 92
Il Re Pastore (Mozart), 16
"Recueillement" (Debussy), 87
regional variations in pronunciation, 26, 31, 48, 125, 126
"Rencontre" (Fauré), 64
resonance: 22; cavities for, 48
rests, 91–92
"Rêve d'amour" (Fauré), 85
Revueltas, Silvestre, 100
Das Rheingold (Wagner), 116, 120, 125, 127, 128, 131, 134, 138
rhythm: 124; pattern of, 25; emphasis in, 144
Rigoletto (Verdi), 12, 13, 14, 16, 18, 27, 29, 31, 34, 35, 36
"Rima" (Turina), 103
Le Roi et le fermier (Monsigny), 86
"Romance" (Debussy), 71, 97
"Romance" (Turina), 102, 103

Roméo et Juliette (Gounod), 50, 51, 52, 69, 75, 90
"Rosemonde" (Chaminade), 83
Der Rosenkavalier (R. Strauss), 107, 111, 113, 121, 124, 133, 136
"Les Roses d'Ispahan" (Fauré), 53, 61, 89
Rossini, Gioacchino, 13, 14, 15, 17, 23, 26, 27, 30, 35, 39
"Ruhe meine Seele" (R. Strauss), 120
Russell, G. Oscar, 9

s: 10, 46; Italian, 26, 27, 31–32, 33, 34, 38, 78; English, 31, 78; German, 31, 78, 121, 132, 134–137, 139, 141; French, 74, 76, 76–78, 83, 87, 89, 96–98; Spanish, 103, 104
s, voiced: 10; Italian, 25–26, 31, 32; French, 58, 60, 76–77, 87, 96; Spanish, 104; German, 125, 141
"Sainte" (Ravel), 85
Saint-Saëns, Camille, 62, 65, 68, 69, 76, 77, 79, 85, 88, 89, 92, 96, 97
Salome (R. Strauss), 116, 131
Samson et Dalila (Saint-Saëns), 62, 65, 68, 69, 77, 79, 88, 92, 97
"Sapphische Ode" (Brahms), 126, 141
"Der Schiffer" (Schubert), 137
"Der Schmied" (Brahms), 122, 136
"Der Scholar" (Wolf), 122, 137
Schubert, Franz, 107, 108, 110, 112, 115, 116, 118, 119, 122, 123, 125, 128, 129,

130, 132, 133, 134, 136, 137, 138, 142, 143, 146
Schumann, Elisabeth, 119
Schumann, Robert, 109, 112, 117, 118, 121, 123, 126, 127, 128, 133, 138, 142, 143
Schwartzkopf, Elisabeth, 119
"Seguidilla murciana" (de Falla), 101, 103, 104, 105
Semet, Théophile, 86
semiconsonants, 15, 66, 125
semiocclusive sounds, 28, 29, 33, 34, 36, 75
semivowels: 4, 8, 11; Spanish, 6; Italian, 6, 14, 18–20, 29, 38–39; French, 6, 48, 66–72, 90; German, 6, 125
separation (hiatus): 18, 39–40; of sounds, 18, 38–44, 67, 72, 91–92, 94, 105, 140, 142, 143–146
"Sérénade" (Bizet), 63, 78
"Sérénade de Molière" (Massenet), 79
"Sérénade Gil Blas" (Semet), 86
sh sound: 10; Italian, 35; English, 35, 135; French, 79–80; German, 135–136, 136, 136–137
shadings, 119, 144
"Si mes vers avaient des ailes" (Hahn), 92
Siebs, Theodor, 106, 139, 140
Siegfried (Wagner), 118, 120, 129, 130, 133, 139

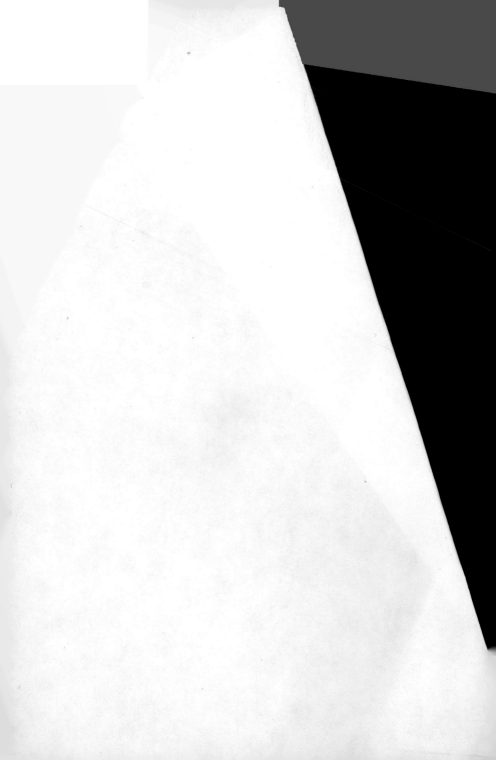